The Innovative Business School

The Innovative Business School formulates a blueprint for the innovative business school of the next decade, with proposed areas of innovation which will train executives to transform the coming technological disruptions into an avenue for world economic development and prosperity.

Offering a new model of business education, the book maps the way forward for business school innovators in exploring questions related to innovation and strategy needed on the part of academic and industry leaders and educators across demographic divides. The chapters cover an overall international and cross-cultural approach in examining the factors at play for business schools of the future and the challenges they face across a range of megatrends affecting today's business environment. The authors impress the need for stakeholders to strategically engage others in the business and education ecosystems through commitment to experimentation, innovation, and sustainable business strategy. Identifying such opportunities for development of a new model for business schools is important to educators and policymakers in preparing to leverage and contribute to existing megatrends to create shared value for regional economies and in new directions.

The Innovative Business School is written for business schools' management and decision-makers, related stakeholders, universities, accreditation agencies, and postgraduate students.

Daphne Halkias, PhD, is a Professor of Management at the International School of Management Paris, a Founding Fellow of the Institute of Coaching at Harvard Medical School, a Research Affiliate at Cornell University and is Editor of the *International Journal of Teaching and Case Studies*.

Michael Neubert, PhD, is a Professor at the International School of Management in Paris, France, where he obtained his PhD and is now also Chair of the Strategic Management Committee. Michael is also a Visiting Professor at Universidad Paraguayo Alemana in San Lorenzo, Paraguay.

Paul W. Thurman, DBA, a Columbia MBA valedictorian, service award winner, and multiple teaching award recipient, has extensive experience helping a variety of governments and corporations realise value from innovative leadership, operations, and technology strategies. Prof. Thurman teaches strategic management and data analysis at Columbia's Mailman School of Public Health.

Chris Adendorff, PhD, is a Futurist Professor at the Nelson Mandela University Business School, International School of Management (France), Ecole des Ponts Business School (France), the University of Johannesburg as well as Trinity University (USA), and is MD of various entrepreneurial ventures in South Africa, Greece, and England.

Sameh Abadir, PhD, is a Professor of Leadership and Negotiation at IMD and co-director of IMD's Negotiating for Value Creation program (NVC). He teaches in IMD's signature program Orchestrating Winning Performance (OWP).

Routledge Focus on Business and Management

The fields of business and management have grown exponentially as areas of research and education. This growth presents challenges for readers trying to keep up with the latest important insights. *Routledge Focus on Business and Management* presents small books on big topics and how they intersect with the world of business.

Individually, each title in the series provides coverage of a key academic topic, whilst collectively, the series forms a comprehensive collection across the business disciplines.

Stories for Management Success
The Power of Talk in Organizations
David Collins

How to Resolve Conflict in Organizations
The Power of People Models and Procedure
Annamaria Garden

Trade Governance of the Belt and Road Initiative
Economic Logic, Value Choices, and Institutional Arrangement
Dawei Cheng

The Innovative Business School
Mentoring Today's Leaders for Tomorrow's Global Challenges
Daphne Halkias, Michael Neubert, Paul W. Thurman, Chris Adendorff and Sameh Abadir

For more information about this series, please visit: www.routledge.com/ Routledge-Focus-on-Business-and-Management/book-series/FBM

The Innovative Business School

Mentoring Today's Leaders for Tomorrow's Global Challenges

Daphne Halkias, Michael Neubert, Paul W. Thurman, Chris Adendorff and Sameh Abadir

LONDON AND NEW YORK

First published 2021

by Routledge
2 Park Square, Milton Park, Abingdon, Oxon OX14 4RN

and by Routledge
52 Vanderbilt Avenue, New York, NY 10017

Routledge is an imprint of the Taylor & Francis Group, an informa business

© 2021 selection and editorial matter, Daphne Halkias, Michael Neubert, Paul W. Thurman, Chris Adendorff and Sameh Abadir; individual chapters, the contributors

British Library Cataloguing-in-Publication Data
A catalogue record for this book is available from the British Library

Library of Congress Cataloging-in-Publication Data
A catalog record has been requested for this book

ISBN: 978-0-367-65029-2 (pbk)
ISBN: 978-0-367-33234-1 (hbk)
ISBN: 978-0-429-31877-1 (ebk)

DOI: 10.4324/9780429318771

Typeset in Times New Roman
by codeMantra

The future of work will be a very different place. So will the future of business schools.

Terence Tse, PhD. Professor at the London campus of ESCP Europe Business School and Co-Founder of Nexus FrontierTech

Contents

Illustrations

Figures

Tables

Contributors

Sameh Abadir, PhD, is a distinguished executive coach and best-selling author in the area of negotiation skills. He is a Professor of Leadership and Negotiation at IMD Business School and Co-Director of IMD's Negotiating for Value Creation program in Lausanne, Switzerland.

Chris Adendorff, PhD, is a Senior Futurist and Presidential Commissioner for the South African Fourth Industrial Revolution and Professor at Nelson Mandela Business School in Port Elizabeth, South Africa.

Peter Bamkole is the Director and Pioneer of Enterprise Development Centre at Pan-Atlantic University in Lagos, Nigeria. He is a PhD candidate at International School of Management Paris.

Tricia Bisoux is Co-Editor of BizEd magazine, which covers insights, trends, and best practices in global business education. BizEd is published by AACSB International, a Florida-based global nonprofit association and accrediting body for collegiate schools of business.

Olivia Choi is an Adjunct Assistant Professor at the Department of Statistics and Actuarial Science, University of Hong Kong. She is a PhD candidate at International School of Management Paris.

Andrew Crisp co-founded CarringtonCrisp in 2003 with Mary Lou Carrington to work with business schools and universities in more than 35 countries across strategy and brand projects and program development. Andrew has spoken widely at industry events organized by EFMD, GMAC, AACSB, the Association of Asia-Pacific Business Schools, CEEMAN, the Canadian Federation of Business School Deans and LinkedIn, while CarringtonCrisp's research has been featured in the *Financial Times, The Economist, The Australian Financial Review, The Globe and Mail,* and many other international publications. The Foreword to our book is a compilation of Andrew's writings, which first appeared in *BizEd Magazine* and *Global Focus: The EFMD Magazine.* He is co-author of CarringstonCrisp's *See the Future* studies supported by The European Foundation for Management Development (EFMD) and The Association for Business Schools (ABS).

Josh Entsminger is an applied researcher in technology and politics. He is currently a doctoral candidate in public sector AI at the Institute for Innovation and Public Purpose at University College London and a Fellow at Nexus FrontierTech.

Mark Esposito, PhD, is a Professor of Economics at Hult International Business School and at Thunderbird School of Global Management at Arizona State University. He has been on the faculty of Harvard University since 2011. He is a Research Associate at Centre for Blockchain Technologies (CBT) at University College London and is Co-Founder of Nexus FrontierTech.

Daphne Halkias, PhD, is a Professor of International Management and Research at International School of Management Paris, a Fellow at Institute of Coaching at McLean Hospital, a Harvard Medical School affiliate. She is a Research Affiliate at the Cornell Center for the Social Sciences, Cornell University, and CEO and Founder of Executive Coaching Consultants.

Aurélie Jean, PhD, is a computational scientist who runs In Silico Veritas, an agency in analytics and computer simulations. Aurélie is an advisor at the BCG and Altermind, a mentor at the FDL at NASA, and an external collaborator for The Ministry of Education of France.

Shefali Nandan, PhD, a distinguished scholar and researcher, is an Assistant Professor on the Faculty of Commerce and Business Administration at University of Allahabad, in Allahabad, India.

Michael Neubert, PhD, is a distinguished researcher and Professor at International School of Management Paris. He is Visiting Professor at Universidad Paraguayo Alemana in San Lorenzo, Paraguay.

Natalia Olynec is a Sustainability Partner and Researcher at IMD Business School, in Lausanne, Switzerland. She is part of the team driving the Sustainability in Family Business Award at IMD Business School and a member of the evaluation committee.

Federico Pigni, PhD, is a Professor at Grenoble Ecole de Management, France, and fellow at the Digital Data Stream Lab at Louisiana State University (LSU). He holds a PhD in Management Information Systems and Supply Chain Management. Before joining Grenoble, he taught at Carlo Cattaneo Unversity - LIUC, Università Commerciale Luigi Bocconi, and the Catholic University in Milan. He was Senior Researcher at LIUC's Lab#ID RFID laboratory and post-doctorate at France Télécom R&D (France). He teaches in the area of Information Systems, and he is currently researching value creation opportunities stemming from big data, digital twins, and 5G networks.

Sharon Shinn is Co-Editor of BizEd magazine, which covers insights, trends, and best practices in global business education. BizEd is published by AACSB International, a Florida-based global nonprofit association and accrediting body for collegiate schools of business.

Mark Smith, PhD, is Dean of Faculty and a Professor at Grenoble Ecole de Management, France, where he leads a faculty of over 150 academics. He was previously Director of the Doctoral School where he managed one of the largest doctoral schools for management sciences in Europe. He led the faculty and school through various accreditations and remains an active researcher with interests in careers, gender, and labor markets.

Paul W. Thurman, DBA, is a distinguished international researcher and consultant in healthcare management and policy, strategic planning, and data analysis, and an Associate Professor in Health Policy and Management at the Columbia University Medical Center and Mailman School of Public Health, Colombia University, New York, USA.

Terence Tse, PhD, a best-selling author in the digital transformation area, is a Professor of Finance at ESCP Europe Business School and Co-Founder of Nexus FrontierTech. He is a Research Associate at Centre for Blockchain Technologies (CBT) at University College London.

Stijn van der Krogt, PhD, is Dean of the Faculty of Business Sciences at Universidad Paraguayo Alemana in San Lorenzo, Paraguay, and Director of Changing Values International in Amsterdam, the Netherlands.

Marta Widz, PhD, embraces the worlds of research, advisory, and practice in the family business field. She is a Research Fellow at IMD Business School, in Lausanne, Switzerland, and heads the evaluation committees of the IMD Global Family Business Award and the Sustainability in Family Business Award at IMD Business School.

Foreword

Time to rethink the MBA—A look into the future

Andrew Crisp

"Reports of my death are greatly exaggerated." These words supposedly uttered by Mark Twain on learning of his obituary being published prematurely could arguably also be said about the MBA degree. Despite headlines announcing that business schools are experiencing declines in their full-time two-year graduate enrollments, the MBA— which remains the flagship program at many business schools—is very much still with us. But what is its future?

Tomorrow's MBA will be changed by new demands from students and employers, evolving technologies, and the entry of alternate providers, to name just a few disruptors. I believe that business schools will need to adapt if they are to continue to attract students and remain relevant—it's time for us to imagine a new MBA. Perhaps the greatest argument for rethinking the MBA is this: If business educators were to imagine a new postgraduate business degree today, few would design a traditional MBA. That's why I expect we'll see more schools completely revamp their MBA degrees. Great opportunities exist for business schools that are willing to redesign their postgraduate portfolios to better meet market demand.

As we look at our research, our first goal is to determine what the data are telling us. Here are just a few of the questions business educators are asking today and the answers we've discovered:

What is driving change? Among the most prominent factors shaping the industry are prospective students' demands for quicker returns, almost instant gratification, and flexible services tailored to their individual needs. According to our research, this trend has resulted in students increasingly preferring one-year MBA programs over two-year formats, as they seek faster and cheaper paths to the degree, as well as a bigger return on their educational investment.

What are employers looking for? Employers' perspective on the MBA is probably the most important factor in determining the future of the degree, and there is evidence that not all MBA programs are developing graduates with the skills that employers want most. For example, one in three employers responding to a 2017 *Financial Times* survey reported that they struggled to find business school graduates with the so-called soft skills, such as the abilities to work with people from a variety of backgrounds, to prioritize tasks, and to manage time well. Employers are making it clear that technical knowledge is not enough—they want people who can work effectively across the organization.

How often will students need to update their skills? The rapid evolution of the workplace means that workers will need to update the skills they develop in their MBA programs sooner rather than later, which could raise doubts about the degree's value. The cost of hiring MBAs also could make them less attractive to employers than applicants with pre-experience master's degrees, who may be viewed as nimbler than MBA graduates. This means that MBA programs must work harder to produce graduates with the flexibility and skills that employers consider critical.

What topics do students value most? Strategy, leadership, and entrepreneurship. In fact, entrepreneurship came in third on the list, its highest rank ever. But that tallies with our data that show that around 25% of MBA students are motivated to start a business at or after graduation. Prospective students also expressed strong preferences for content related to marketing, international business, project management, economics, technology management, data analysis, and decision-making.

What are the biggest competitors to the MBA? In the business school sector, the popularity of the MBA is giving way to the rise of specialist master's programs, which offer students more flexibility, lower prices, and degrees that are increasingly recognized by employers. Specialized programs are providing the market with a serious alternative to the MBA. Schools must be careful to make the master's and MBA programs in their portfolios complementary offerings, rather than programs that conflict with or cannibalize each other. Outside the sector, competition comes from organizations such as consultancies, corporate universities, and the tech sector. For example, LinkedIn launches 30 or more new courses each week as part of a course library that now extends to more than 10,000 different programs. In the future, students could turn to such self-paced, just-in-time educational options in greater numbers.

Perhaps the biggest question for business schools involves just how they should respond to these ongoing trends. While each school has its own strengths, values, and objectives, all business schools can take the following strategies to heart as they consider their next steps:

Embrace more flexible program formats. When I was growing up, there were only three channel choices on British television, and they all were delivered across the same platform. Today, there are thousands of choices, some delivered via traditional means to my television, but others bypassing television altogether, delivered via streaming services to my laptop, tablet, and smartphone. The MBA is moving in the same direction. In our research, 43% of prospective students cite program flexibility as a big factor in where they choose to study. That's why it is rare today to see a business school offer an MBA through just one mode of delivery. Instead, schools offer specialist, executive, part-time, weekend, online, and blended formats. Some MBA programs don't require students to set foot on a traditional campus; others allow students to study at their own pace; others allow students to personalize content, study remotely, or access material over mobile devices.

Be open to collaboration. The challenge for schools is finding business models that enable multiple approaches to the MBA, which aren't always compatible with how a business school is structured. Collaboration is one way to provide students with greater choice. By working with faculties in a parent university or external organizations, schools can offer a wider variety of MBA program formats and delivery methods.

Invest in soft skills development. Like respondents to the *Financial Times* skills survey, a quarter of the prospective MBA students we surveyed noted that they wanted to develop their skills in leadership, communication, and critical thinking. More than one in five respondents wanted to strengthen their entrepreneurial mindsets, team building and teamwork skills, and networking and collaboration skills.

Consider specialist MBA programs. With today's students seeking out MBA programs that are relevant and targeted to their career goals, business schools might also consider tailoring their MBA programs to suit specific industries. We've seen an increase in specialist MBAs, such as the Real Madrid MBA in Sports Management at Escuela Universitaria Real Madrid Universidad Europea in Spain, a degree delivered in partnership with the Real Madrid football club; or the Thoroughbred Horse Racing Industries MBA at the University of Liverpool in the United Kingdom. Students interested in entering careers in the wine industry, the energy sector, healthcare management, luxury brand management, or sustainability all can seek out MBAs focused on these particular fields. Areas of greatest student interest include information technology, finance, and entrepreneurship.

Design more personalized career services. Ultimately, most students enroll in MBA programs because they want to advance into more senior roles at their organizations or move their careers into new sectors. In "Tomorrow's MBA," 25% of prospective students noted that they placed special value on four types of professional development: career coaching, career development workshops, personalized career planning, and mentorship programs. Schools can design such highly personalized services to differentiate themselves from competitors.

When it comes to the future of the MBA, there will be no prizes for being in the middle. Demand for the MBA isn't disappearing, but schools that lack strong brands, flexible offerings, nimble content, personalized services, or reputations in particular industry sectors are likely to feel a squeeze. At the end of 2012, the *New York Times* published an article titled "Year of the MOOC". While the MOOC revolution may not have panned out as some people anticipated, by the end of 2017, Coursera had registered 30 million learners and as a business was reportedly valued at $800 million. The Babson Survey Research Group in its 2017 report found that distance student enrolments in the US have increased for 14 years in a row. And growing. Beyond technology, 70% of managers in businesses who responded to the *See the Future* studies survey agreed that business models need to change to better engage with society.

Turmoil is probably too strong a word but "uncertain" may not be strong enough to describe the landscape that business schools are operating in today. Much has been written and many conference speeches given about the impact on business schools of the global financial crisis, growing international competition, the importance of sustainability and ethics, and more recently the likely impact of new technologies. Despite suggestions about business schools finding themselves on the edge of the crevasse, most have avoided taking the plunge. There have been some large-scale failures in the US, especially in the for-profit sector, and mergers continue elsewhere, but there has been no collapse. Some full-time MBA programs have closed but others thrive, especially in Asia. Around the world, there are also many examples of innovation in business education with providers not only surviving but growing significantly.

So, what of the next five years? Recent media coverage of business, whether it has been the performance of the banks, chief executives of car companies using executive jets when their businesses are failing, youth unemployment in the eurozone, or even cities going bankrupt in the US, will undoubtedly influence perceptions, especially among young people. Given the interest in changing business models and moving away from shareholder value, it is not surprising that more than 80% of respondents in the *See the Future* studies survey agree that "sustainability and ethics should be embedded in all business education programmes".

Many schools have already introduced ethics and sustainability modules to their business programs, but the demand from both employers and students is that these subjects be a seamless part of the curriculum whether students are studying finance, marketing, HR, or any other aspect of business. Of course, before thinking about curriculum, schools need to consider what attracts students to them. Just under half of all respondents in the *See the Future* study agree that "schools that don't teach sustainability, corporate social responsibility and ethics should be ranked lower than those that do". Money remains important, especially given the high fees associated with many business degree programs. However, the study suggests that more students value a business education as a way to a more fulfilling job rather than a more highly paid one.

For many graduates, employment may also have an international dimension whether that means working overseas or simply dealing with international organizations and companies. Over the last 20 years, internationalism has become an accepted part of a business school's offer, delivering little by way of differentiation from competitor schools. So, what do students and employers really want when they talk about internationalism? To start with, more than two-thirds of all current and prospective students would be interested in studying abroad for all or part of their degree. The US remains the most popular destination, with the UK second, but Singapore and China are on the rise, ranking fourth and sixth, respectively, with many respondents. If your business school is in a city which shares the same name as a Premier League football club, that's an awful lot of name awareness when a student starts searching Google.

Of course, few decide where to study based on a football team, but when in conversation about global brands with young people in China and the first three spontaneous answers are Nokia, Manchester United, and David Beckham, the power of sport becomes clearer. Employers perhaps have a less emotional view of how internationalism should fit into a business school. Almost all agree that a good business education should develop an understanding of business in different parts of the world. Interestingly, though, just over a third of all managers and directors also agree that "graduates should learn another language as part of their degree". Increasingly that language learning might be delivered via technology, perhaps utilizing native speakers at the end of a Skype connection rather than lecturers in the classroom. And it is technology, especially MOOCs (massive open online courses), which currently account for much of the discussion about the future in business schools.

The generation entering business schools today has grown up with digital technology. It is a core part of their lives. They expect it to be a part of education and understand it offers the opportunity not just to enhance the classroom experience but for lifestyle learning around their other commitments. Where technology and learning seem likely to have a greater impact in the short term is in informal settings as well as the workplace. Over 70% of prospective students, current students and alumni want lifestyle learning, using technology to learn without disrupting work and family commitments. Delivered via video and podcasts or through apps on a smartphone or tablet, technology offers the opportunity for "anytime-anywhere learning" with students getting taster sessions or the chance to bring skills up to date.

Predicting the future is a difficult business. Should a business school focus on money or fulfillment, China or Chicago, sustainability or shareholder value, on-campus or online? There is yet another option—some schools could opt to take larger risks to gain "first-mover advantage," a well-known concept among startups. The first to market with a new product or service gains momentum by leading the industry. This begs the question: Who will be the first movers among today's MBA providers? What will MBA programs of the future look like? Most likely, they will allow students to regularly update their learning. They will provide flexible formats that adapt quickly to the needs of students and employers. They will put what students learn in the context of wider societal issues, and they will leverage technology to enhance and deliver strong student experiences that go far beyond the academic into the experiential.

Imagine that.

Part 1

Innovating the business school

The Fourth Industrial Revolution started in 2012. It will bring about unprecedented change and as a society we are now entering unchartered territory.

The complexity and plurality of industrial revolution 4.0 includes advances in artificial intelligence (AI), the internet of things (IoT), and blockchain technology.

It is now globally recognized that industrial revolution 4.0 represents a fundamental change in the way we live, work, and relate to each other. It is inevitable that, as with any revolution, change will occur in desirable and undesirable ways.

The effects of the change of this revolution are already evident in the way in which societies produce, distribute, and consume the full range of goods and services that underpin human existence, and which drive human development. However, there are considerable differences in the pace of change within different socio-technical systems and between different countries. A particular area of intense change is in production systems.

By 2030, over two billion jobs as we know them today will have disappeared, freeing up talent for many and new industrial revolution 4.0 fledgling industries, with many opportunities to the innovation sector and their creators, fundamentally changing the nature of work.

As industrial revolution 4.0 rule of thumb, 60% of jobs that will exist toward the end of 2030 have not yet been conceived of or invented.

Toward 2030, basic computer programming will be considered a core skill required in over 30% of future industries and work.

Futurists predict that humankind will experience more changes in our immediate future, than our combined history put together.

Implementing the research actions orientated toward the Fourth Industrial Revolution requires substantial stakeholder participation, as well as cross-sectoral cooperation within the cultural and creative industries.

By 2030, a surge of microtraining colleges and institutions will spring to life, as part of educating the future workforce. Each will require less than six months training and apprentices to prepare us in switching or adapting to our professions.

In a time of extraordinary change, every individual, business, industry, and government are being impacted by breakthroughs in computing power, connectivity, AI, biotechnology, and other innovative technologies—this is a revolution without boundaries, spreading across the world with incredible velocity. The Fourth Industrial Revolution is here and it is real. What is most important for educators is how it is to be harnessed and carried to future leaders to the greater benefit of all.

So, where does all this leave the more than 16,000 business schools worldwide training tomorrow's leaders today?

We offer our response in this first part of *The Innovative Business School*.

1 Introduction: will business schools be the disrupter or the disrupted?

Our book was developed as a blueprint for the innovative business school of the next decade, where professors train executives to transform the coming technological disruptions into an avenue for world economic development and prosperity. The specific need for the book arose from the problem that opportunities identified in the literature as a result of this process are broad and do not offer a specific prescription for success. Business schools must consider a range of megatrends affecting today's business environment, with foremost that of the human demographics, innovation, sustainable development, and technology driving the Fourth Industrial Revolution (industrial revolution 4.0).

Industrial revolution 4.0 poses risks to the political, economic, and social fabric of all countries and communities (Adendorff & Putzier, 2018). It will mean significant changes as well as challenges for governments, businesses, civil society organizations, and the media. Davis (2012) indicated that one of the most intense impacts of the industrial revolution 4.0 will be on the jobs people have and the skills that are necessary for success. From the perspective of emerging economies, this is of particular concern considering the high level of unemployment in the country (Adendorff & Putzier, 2018). Any further job losses will have a severe impact on tax revenues; pension funds will be affected, and it is probable that the social damage as a far-reaching result of lost taxes, lost employment, and lower gross domestic product (GDP) will increase (Burda, 2015).

Davis (2012) also mentions that a hallmark of globalized, dematerialized markets is the trend to assign massive rewards to "stars", that is, individuals, products, or businesses who, either through fluke or distinctive talent, gain early and pervasive attention at the cost of those less fortunate or not quite as talented. At the same time, the very presence of global platforms to facilitate such dissemination, along with reduced transactional costs, also suggests substantial gains for those who own the platforms and connected infrastructure and further generates new fears for aggravated inequality within countries (Davis, 2012). One such example is WhatsApp, which created extraordinary returns for a small group of creators and investors when Facebook agreed to pay USD 22 billion for the company, which then consisted of just 55 employees, in February 2014 (Baweja, Donovan, Haefele, Siddiqi, & Smiles, 2016).

The capacity of business schools to change within industrial revolution 4.0 will govern their survival; in order to preserve their competitive edge, business schools must prove proficient in embracing a realm of disruptive revolution and either expose their structures to new levels of efficiency and transparency or face growing discontent. Given the speed of change and far-reaching impacts, business schools across the globe are being challenged to an unparalleled point not just for purposes of educating tomorrow's leaders, but for their very survival. Our book is taking a futures methodology approach to systematically explore, recommend, and propose both desirable and possible future visions to assist in the creation of a new kind of business school. The innovative business school will have long-term policies, plans, and strategies for constantly redesigning their curriculum to convey training and knowledge in close alignment with the world business school graduates will be called upon to build in the coming years. Possibly the most generally understood purpose of futures method is to aid in identifying what you don't know, but must know, in order to make more intelligent choices. Before educating the students, business school leaders and faculty must prepare themselves to prepare adequately and have a clear grasp of how the Fourth Industrial Revolution might shape the worldwide economy and society into the next decade.

Developed and developing societies are currently informed by two guiding models, namely the 'science' (or knowledge-based) society and the 'sustainable' society. The science society is predominantly driven by the megatrends of 'scientific and technological innovations, knowledge transfer, qualification, and education' (Kreibich, Oertel, & Wölk, 2012). In order to gain a competitive advantage in this fast-changing world, it is imperative that business schools embrace their role in shaping the leaders of tomorrow's global economy and megatrend challenges today. It is scientific discovery and technological innovation, forces of nature, and social and political dynamics that essentially determine the future; however, it is mankind's choices that progressively shape it. While future-oriented work like our book is concerned about learning and looking at new insights to achieve a variety of different ends (Iversen, 2006), the purpose of futures research is to help inform insights, choices, and alternatives concerning the future.

From a theoretical perspective, our ideas and visions within this book were guided by the theoretical research frameworks within disruptive innovation theory (Christensen, Raynor, & McDonald, 2015). Markides (2006) and King and Baatartogtokh (2015) interpreted Christensen's (1992) original notion of "the innovator's dilemma", which eventually morphed into a theory of disruptive innovation (Christensen, Raynor, & McDonald, 2015), by stating that disruptive innovation concepts are 'new to the world products' or 'business model innovations' not just technical innovations. Disruptive innovation theory in terms of education consists of extending knowledge to allow academics to be the driver for creating improved access to high-quality education, designing personalized education, and circumnavigating the politics of education, while deciding what needs to be taught and how (Arnett, 2014).

Disruptive innovation theory can be applied in understanding and making recommendation for building innovative MBA programs on data from relevant research questions addressing today's challenges of the global marketplace such as gender-related issues, digital entrepreneurship. AI, technology diffusion in developing economies, and the impact of business on economic development and sustainability (Anderson, Ellwood, & Coleman, 2017; Dover, Manwani, & Munn, 2018). Today's business schools must strategically engage others in the business and education ecosystems, by a commitment to experimentation, innovation, and sustainable business strategy (Horn & Dunagan, 2018). This is a vision for a future where the innovative business school of the next decade changes the narrative about the role of business education as well as that of business in society (AACSB, 2018). Therefore, this book will attempt to offer a future vision of business education and map the way forward for business school innovators in answering the following central research question: *What areas of innovation and strategy must be addressed by business school leaders and educators to support a new model of business education which trains executives to transform today's technological and market disruptions into an avenue for world economic development and prosperity across demographic divides?*

In identifying opportunities into a new model for the MBA curriculum, it is important to business educators to seize upon existing megatrends evolving regional economies in new directions. One comment we often heard from business students around the world is the tug of war within their faculty between those with outdated knowledge and those with teaching models based on megatrends stemming from industrial revolution 4.0. Today's business schools must strategically engage others in the business and education ecosystems, by a commitment to experimentation and innovation not just in student learning but first and foremost in teaching. This is a vision for a future where the business school redesigns both its mission and curriculum to change the narrative about the role of business education, and of business, in society. For business schools to transform into centers of learning and training for leaders facing tomorrow's local and global challenges, first their own faculty must comprise educators and mentors whose teaching, research, and professional practice revolve around the megatrends of the next decade.

In developing our forecasting of megatrends to affect business school teaching models, we first looked to those explored by world-renowned professors and thought leaders Terence Tse and Mark Esposito in their 2017 ground-breaking book: *Understanding How the Future Unfolds: Using Drive to Harness the Power of Today's Megatrends.* Tse and Esposito's scholarly work offers a holistic way to think about tomorrow by preparing for it today in a framework they named *DRIVE*, which examined five interrelated megatrends for the future: demographic and social changes, resource scarcity, inequalities, volatility, complexity, and scale and enterprising dynamics. Within these complex topics, we extended the range of megatrends business schools can consider affecting today's business environment when developing innovative training programs for tomorrow's leaders, as we visualize in Figure 1.1: the internet of everything (IoE), blockchain technology, urbanization solutions, cashless and alternative forms of financing, convergence and connectivity, smart security, green business solutions, social trends defined through the United Nations' 17 Sustainable Development Goals (SDGs), smart cities, automation, the future of mobility, and AI.

As per all the previous revolutions, industrial revolution 4.0 we find at our doorstep is about disruption, not only for individuals, but for business as well. Production was automated in the First Industrial Revolution; electric power for mass production was used in the second; and, in the third, information technology was used to automate production (Falcioni, 2016). Now, industrial revolution 4.0 is characterized by its exponential evolution, and unlike the three previous industrial revolutions (IRs), it is not purely linear (Bloem, Doorn, Duivestein, Excoffier, Maas, & Ommeren, 2014). While the increasing use of technology can be seen daily, the industrial revolution 4.0's bearing on other aspects of the economy has to be critically assessed. In the paper *Impact of Technological Innovations on the Social Structure*, Dmitriev, Kalinicheva, Shadoba, Nikonets, Pogonysheva and Shvarova (2016) highlighted the negative consequences of innovations, which could lead to the displacement of human labor by automated systems.

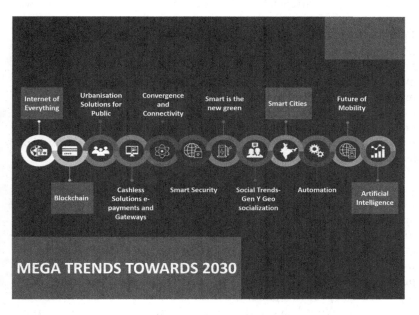

Figure 1.1 Megatrends within the Fourth Industrial Revolution toward 2030.

The challenge and responsibility to manage the industrial revolution 4.0's potential and advancing effects on economic policy and society lie in the hands of governments and the private sectors alike, whose leaders are today's students in the more than 16,000 business schools worldwide (Adendorff & Putzier, 2018).

Industrial revolution 4.0 will no doubt change the way humankind lives, works, and relates to one another. We are experiencing change at a speed unlike anything the world has experienced before, which compels us to live and create realities that were previously unthinkable (Adendorff, 2018). The rapid and vast changes we are beginning to experience in both our personal and professional lives call for a drastic shift in our thinking patterns and the way in which every industry will need to conduct business in the near future. Not only will business models in each and every trade need to transform in order to meet the growing needs and demands of consumers, but—more importantly—we will need to make a shift in the way we see and experience the world, and as educators be equipped to pass this vision onto our students in business schools. If the teacher is not a learner, the student will just be left behind no matter how much knowledge is thrown their way.

Our book is written for the teachers and mentors of tomorrow's leaders, those of us who set the standard for learning in more than 16,000 institutions around the world granting business qualifications (Pitt-Watson & Quigley, 2019). We are fed new and innovative thinking and practice in business school on a daily basis via social media, primarily the top 30 business schools around the globe. Yet, let's keep in mind that the majority of business students globally are not at those 30 top-tier, well-funded, competitive business schools. If we only depend on the thought leaders in those top 30 business schools to produce the innovators of tomorrow's world, then we forget those who live and lead in millions of communities worldwide.

Today, as a global society, we face daunting social, economic, and environmental challenges outlined in the United Nations' SDGs, which if not addressed may have cataclysmic results to our planet. The processes by which business schools may reimagine their curriculum to address these global sustainability challenges have emerged as recommendations for research in scholarly literature, yet few published works have tackled these issues in one package. As researchers and professors ourselves, we have reviewed thousands of sources on this topic over the past two years. Our aim with this book is to synthesize our collective knowledge and experience into a blueprint developing the innovative business school we need now. We want to offer our colleagues a thoughtful, holistic, architectural design that may inspire business school leaders, educators, and practitioners in transforming today's business schools as centers of learning and action in tackling the pressing global challenges of our times.

2 The evolution of business schools: past and present

Higher education is in a time of transition, and colleges and universities alike are struggling to keep pace. This effect is particularly seen in schools where their pedagogical foundations are evolving so quickly—and so dramatically—that adapting curricula, faculty, and support resources is a daily challenge. This is most visibly seen, perhaps, in business schools where challenges come from a number of external factors:

- Changing student populations (new generations, cultures, attitudes)
- Emerging and evolving labor market and workplace demands
- New technologies and research on learning methods and pedagogy
- New market and societal "shocks"; e.g., climate change, social media, sustainability

In addition, several internal forces at work are also affecting the efficiency and efficacy at which business schools can adapt to these exogenous trends and adopt new internal mechanisms to meet them:

- Reduced public and grant/research funding, given strained public budgets
- Declining revenues, given relative inabilities to raise prices, given escalating costs (particularly for in-person delivery models)
- Competition from new entrants and disruptors that look nothing like a traditional college or university

To better understand how business schools—and perhaps higher education institutions, more generally—have gotten to this point, some historical perspective will be helpful. By seeing how business schools have arrived at this critical point in their life cycles, they may be able to chart a clearer course forward not only to ensure a better match with what rapidly markets are demanding but also to ensure that they remain going concerns—as businesses and as producers of the next generation of business leaders—for many years ahead.

Business school beginnings

Although formal business school education has existed since the early 19th century, competition among them—and notable business leaders from them—started to appear in the mid to late 20th century after World War II as many nations became more industrialized and academic studies and disciplines emerged that focused on business leadership, management, operations, and decision-making. Prior to the prevalence of undergraduate and graduate business degrees, most notably the Master of Business Administration (or MBA), many business leaders came from schools focused on engineering, applied sciences, and, in many cases, law. Having a background in legal studies ostensibly meant a manager or leader could negotiate, make decisions, agree to contracts, and effectively promote interests of a firm to potential investors, shareholders, and business partners.

As more business studies and scholarship were conducted, these disparate disciplines—from operations management, accounting, finance, marketing, and decision sciences—began to make sense as a singular focus of study, academic prestige, and faculty classification. As business schools then began to emerge, they began to create research in business disciplines—and in focused business scholarship journals—and turn out graduates who were better prepared to face real-life "general management" challenges often seen in firms, companies, and corporations. These trained business leaders, then, would hire into firms at higher levels, rise more quickly, and also feed more prospective students back into the business school system as the reputations and successes of these trained businesspeople continued to prosper.

Of course, the challenges present in the middle of the 20th century were significant. Mass production, industrialization, public capital markets, and the emergence of various funding mechanisms to support rapid advances in business demanded a set of managers and leaders who had exposure and training in such challenges and methods prior to entering the corporate world. And once undergraduates with business training became common in the job market and professional workforce, those with some business experience also sought to gain more advanced leadership skills. As such postgraduate degrees became popular—like the MBA or Master degree in Management—along with some popular derivative degrees such as those in public administration and management, real estate, manufacturing and operations, and finance. Business degree programs essentially mimicked the corporate "siloes" that were quite evident in firms at the time: accounting/finance, marketing, manufacturing/operations, strategic planning (often referred to simply as "management"), and human resources or "industrial management." Even today, most business schools— including many of the world's elite ones—have departmental structures that replicate these business functions or "stovepipes."

However, corporate-management structures and theories have changed dramatically since the mid to late 20th century. Few employees work in single physical locations and even fewer commit to long careers with just one or two firms. Service industries are much more common than pure manufacturing ones, and firms are much more global in nature and depend on partnerships and alliances to add value (instead of conglomeration). Financing of firm operations can take on myriad forms and structures, now, as can workforces with renewed emphasis on diversity and inclusion. Managing people is much less hierarchical, more team-based, and project-driven, not department-driven, and more professional jobs require cross-functional skills; e.g., marketers who understand information technology, product managers who value and promote services, also, and financial leaders who have deeper understanding of customer needs and relationships. Even the "personnel" function—now "talent management"—has transitioned from being a purely hiring-focused role to one that involves hiring, placement, ongoing training and career pathing, employee wellness and benefits, ombudsman ship and conflict resolution, outsourcing, and exit planning (to assist workers have graceful exits whether they've been terminated or wish to leave voluntarily).

And needless to say, technology in the workplace is much different/more advanced and changing much more rapidly, today, than it did in the mid to late 20th century. Workplaces are now mobile-enabled, employees have a variety of handheld and mobile devices to connect them to work and to each other, and the demands of customers and stakeholders reach far beyond the 9am-to-5pm routine common decades ago. And new technologies are entering the workplace at a blistering pace. Artificial intelligence, machine learning, social media, augmented reality, online-only business models, "gig" economies that are tech-enabled, and omnichannel everything—giving customers what they want, when they want it, however they choose to receive it—have had huge economic and social impacts—to suppliers and demanders, alike—in just the past few years.

But business schools have found it difficult to keep up. Paradoxically, business schools have become quite successful at addressing current business challenges based on history, yet we also demand that these same business schools train the business leaders, today, to face emerging challenges in the future (Alajoutsijärvi, Juusola, & Siltaoja, 2015). Thus, some find it ironic that business schools may teach courses on innovation and design thinking, for example, but that the schools, themselves, find it nearly impossible to innovate at the speed of the businesses they purport to support (Çeviker-Çınar, Mura, & Demirbağ-Kaplan, 2017).

Defining standards and quality

To be clear, though, business schools and their leaders have not just "shot from the hip" for decades trying anything and everything to become "good." Schools and their universities—as well as outside adjudicators of excellence in education—have developed standards for goodness in business education over time. Several accreditation bodies—the Accreditation Council for Business Schools and Programs (ACBSP), The Association to Advance Collegiate Schools of Business (AACSB), and International Accreditation Council for Business Education (IACBE)—accredit most schools in the United States, whereas the EFMD Quality Improvement System (EQUIS) system is used in Europe as are standards by the Association of MBAs (AMBA) (for MBA programs) and the Business Graduates Association (BGA) for business schools.

However, like the curricula at their accredited schools, these accreditation bodies have found it difficult to keep up with emerging demands and needs for business education in the rapidly moving digital age. Concepts such as cybersecurity, social media business modeling, business continuity and risk management, and management of cross-border organizations and public–private partnerships are all just now being considered as assessment criteria for future business administration programs.

This has led some scholars and business leaders to question the structure and futures of existing business education—not only in terms of what is delivered but also how such delivery is managed by the schools and universities, themselves. Traditional top-down leadership and tenure-based faculty promotion are in the crosshairs as such leadership and scholarship management do not always lead to innovative curricular and business school "business model" successes. Calls to change the "DNA" of business education—and to be more disruptive in the ways business schools think about what they offer to their marketplaces—have become more common, and some scholars and industry observers note that if not careful, business schools are on the precipice of losing touch with the "realities" of their student and hiring firm needs and may risk losing academic legitimacy, too, if significant structural changes are not realized.

Criticism, skepticism, and funding challenges

Of course, if business academies lose touch with student realities—and with hiring firm needs and market demands—then funding for them will surely suffer. If schools do not teach the right skills or address what employers want, then the fundamental business models of business schools will be called into question. Today, schools are largely funded by student tuition, public and private grants (for those schools that focus on business and management research and scholarship), philanthropy, and partnerships with corporate sponsors (sometimes benefactors). Students (and sometimes firms) pay tuition, funders provide grants, the school's development office raises funds from charitable giving, and corporate sponsors provide some capital but also are the key source of "pull" for business school graduates: jobs.

However, if schools do not quickly adapt to the needs of these employers, this rather simple business model is ripe for disruption (Peters, Thomas, & Smith, 2018). In fact, distance learning programs, non-degree and executive education academies, and internal corporate "universities" are already making schools quickly rethink what "businesses" they are actually in (Peters, Smith, & Thomas, 2018). But this rethinking requires business schools to admit some of their deficiencies and to rethink (and to tear down and to rebuild) their basic infrastructures, including the buildings they use, the faculty they hire, and the curricula they teach. This openness to criticism is not natural—especially among elite schools—and transparency of these business models is not something that the schools or their universities naturally promote.

Out of sync ... or out of touch: legitimacy and the future

In addition, some business schools are seen to be out of touch with society since curricula and educational programs—not to mention faculty research in some areas—are quite far behind modern trends and challenges faced by new managers and leaders graduating from these programs. Technology and globalization, alone, have "squeezed" good managerial jobs yet many business schools may be ignoring these trends or at least not updating their curricula quickly enough to adapt to them. Even the ethics being taught in today's business curricula are often accused of being behind the times since few are addressing social needs such as poverty.

Recalling an earlier example, some business schools have embraced recent curricular concepts such as disruptive innovation and agile management in digital businesses. However, even if graduates learn these concepts and deploy them upon graduation, are there other key disciplines—or interdisciplinary studies—that will better prepare them for real challenges in more globalized, multi-polar contexts? Adding a few "hot topics" courses may provide Band-Aids to some curricula, but without full integration of these key, emerging business themes and tools, business schools will continue to struggle for preference among employers and, in some cases, may risk losing funding if not seen as more "current" in their markets. To be clear, some colleges and universities are setting new trends in emerging areas, but more business schools need to be more disruptively ... or risk disruption, themselves, from competition that looks nothing like traditional business school delivery models, faculty, or curricula.

Emerging spaces, places, and business models

To be clear, however, not only the curricula need to change in order for business schools to successfully—and to continually—adapt to emerging trends and needs. Schools need to carefully rethink how, when, and where business education needs to be delivered. Presence learning is declining; in-person MBA programs are shutting down in favor of distance learning and online programs. This will require new teaching and pedagogical methods to address these 21st-century knowledge gaps. Teaching and learning in the digital era are different and require different methods, techniques, and infrastructure to be effective not to mention support for new ways of ensuring quality and continued innovation over time.

In addition, the underlying business models of how business education is taught, distributed, and "monetized" will also require reexamination, including how a business academy defines its culture and how it focuses on its "customers." In fact, more and more business schools are partnering and allying in order to offer such diverse, global experiences, and these "network models" of learning may show promise as long as curricula are equally innovative. However, as more "open" curricula are proffered (massive open online courses, or MOOCs, free online academies, etc.), these will put even more pressure on the business models of traditional business schools while at the same time forcing potentially expensive retrofitting of their portfolios for their ever-global institutional and individual partners. One specific example of such a challenge is the emerging—and very fast-moving and rapidly changing—world of financial technology. Given the global nature of this business area—not to mention the incredibly rapid pace of technological innovation in this space—business schools are having difficulties even settling on how to best serve this needy market for business leaders with coding, financial, global, and technology skillsets.

The only constant: change

But even if business schools and academies—traditional and emerging—could simply snap their fingers and instantly match their "supply" of educational services, technology, and scholarship with the immediate demands of employers' and students' "demand" for the same, these curricula, faculty, delivery models, and business set-ups would be, at best, valid for only a heartbeat. Although many corporate finance curricula still focus on large, fixed-cost, asset-based, mostly one-country-based businesses, much of the rest of the business world has bypassed these models years ago. So, even if we could make it all good and proper, tomorrow, what's not to say that in another year or so, all of our work would need to be reimagined, reinvented, and retooled.

Emerging business issues such as climate change, renewable energy and markets, sustainability, and improved transparency and corporate governance are the next—and perhaps, now, most current—business challenges that emerging managers, leaders, and graduates must tackle to be successful. Globalization is already thought of in many business circles as a foregone conclusion as are diversity of workforces, boundaryless or borderless trade and labor portability, and not just the use but the dependence on technology to prosecute even the simplest of business models. However, many business schools still have faculty, curricula, and programs essentially "stuck" in a business world of old and find it quite difficult to pivot to these new demands (even though these same schools teach and preach disruptive innovation, adaptive and agile business models, and circular economic principles, daily!).

Business academies must, for example, embrace sustainability and lead the charge for the next generation of business leaders and executives. This requires instructional methods that are less didactic, less "case-based," and more creative and cultivating in nature. In fact, some scholars have gone on to say that we no longer need "managers" coming out of our business schools; instead, we need creative thinker and "imaginators," instead. These needs highlight the real challenge that business schools have: how to learn and forecast needed skills and trends and to become leading indicators, themselves, of what is to come, as opposed to reactive agents that teach "yesterday's skills" to today's leaders. This is clearly not easy as seen in recent struggles schools have had simply defining and agreeing to what it means to incorporate "sustainability" into management and business curricula.

But make no mistake: even if universities and schools can address these challenges today—and define what a business school of the future might look like—they know the only constant, and constant struggle, is change. And change not only affects curricula and faculty but also the very fabric of the business model(s) upon which the school operates and pays its bills. Indeed, more shocks will come, technologies will evolve and change, and new entrants and disruptors will certainly try to extract value from slow-to-adapt business academies. And consumers (students and employers) and suppliers (universities and their faculties) will quickly move—perhaps more quickly than ever before—to those who provide the right training at the right time for the right challenges. Business schools have preached "change management" for decades, but now is the time for the academies to provide change leadership before disruption puts the VHS tapes of some business curricula, faculty, and programs on the same shelf as Blockbuster.

"Disrupt or be disrupted" is a very contemporary battle cry, now, for business school leaders. Incremental changes to courses and curricula are likely not sufficient to address the ever-changing needs from learners and hiring firms, especially when these needs are no longer just in the course catalog. How and where people learn, how much they are willing to pay, and how long they are willing to wait to complete a course of study are all being challenged, now. And the technologies they use and employ—both to learn and to work—have never been changing and advancing as rapidly.

3 Transforming the MBA curriculum for industrial revolution 4.0

As we enter the Fourth Industrial Revolution (industrial revolution 4.0 or 4IR), the demand for education, economic development, and sustainable livelihoods across the globe has never been higher. The calls to action for business education to align its mission with managing the social and economic upheaval coming with the advent of artificial intelligence (AI) and technological innovation make business schools easy targets for disruption and innovation. Business schools find themselves at a crossroads between educating students to work in tomorrow's world and challenging the industries that support them to reform their missions. Business school leaders are called on to reflect on how business education delivered to thousands of students daily can remain relevant in addressing challenges facing both society and the business community, and train those students to reinvent themselves every three to five years.

The term 'industrial revolution' is used to refer to the transformation of the social and technological economic systems in industry, focusing in particular on changes in living conditions, circumstances of work, and economic wealth (Dombrowski & Wagner, 2014). The First Industrial Revolution mechanized production, the second one used electric power for mass manufacturing, and the third used information technology to automate production. It seems the 4IR will distort the lines between the digital, the physical, and the biological realms (Falcioni, 2016). While the earlier industrial revolutions were driven by swift developments in connectivity and automation, beginning with the technologies that launched the First Industrial Revolution in 18th-century England, through to the exponential increases in the computing power of modern times, the 4IR is similarly driven by the same two forces—automation and connectivity (Baweja, Donovan, Haefele, Siddiqi, & Smiles, 2016; Newbigin, 2017). According to Schwab (2017), this revolution comes on the back of a number of transformative technologies, but it is, at the same time, much more than the sum of all those technologies. Contrary to belief, the 4IR started to take effect in 2012 (World Economic Forum, 2017; Adendorff & Putzier, 2018).

Critics insist that after business schools unleashed their graduates to create a global financial crisis in the previous decade. The time has now come for business schools to transform their models of learning and broaden their students' training to address how the business community can participate in meeting economic, environmental, and social challenges for all populations around the world. Such a transformation is slowly starting to gain momentum in business schools around the world, offering the Master of Business Administration degree, more commonly known as the MBA. For business schools to graduate individuals equipped to meet the demands of the 21st-century workforce, they need to reform their models of and approaches to executive education, including the currently prevailing MBA paradigm.

The problem is universities worldwide describe their MBA programs as 'transformative,' yet so many of these are rooted in structures, curricula, and methods of assessment that are mostly retrospective, and they have come under heavy criticism for failing to properly train leaders to successfully navigate the Fourth Industrial Revolution. The recent fast pace of innovation has enabled the reinvention of entire industries in a few short years, and some even just months, rather than progressively over the decades. Estimates of the degree to which the economy will transform over the next 10–20 years include projections that by 2035 half of all current jobs will no longer exist, and about the same percentage of future jobs will be entirely new. Disruption, scaled-up from the perspective of the employee to that of the employer, whether on account of the 'gig' economy, big data and data analytics, value chain disaggregation, or even only due to innovation, is also imminent. Business-to-consumer industries, which category business schools belong to, will bear the greatest brunt, with industry slated to follow soon after.

For many in academia, the MBA degree is now more about prestige than transformation, despite clear indications that the global economy is at a watershed mark as a result of the significant ecosystem changes already taking place. Current demands on organizations to advance in innovation and learning are a worldwide and well-grounded concern. Scholars and thought leaders in education have concluded that business schools, as critical providers of executives into the global marketplace through their MBA programs, produce graduates who cannot, for the more significant part, be innovative in meeting today's global development challenges as outlined by the World Economic Forum.

Technology is having a distinctive impact on business, forcing changes to the hitherto accepted nature and notion of work as well as the role of managers. At the same time, technology is also producing uncertainty regarding the future character of jobs and the skills required to perform them successfully.

Increasingly, success at the organizational level calls for creative and flexible employees who can drive, shape, and lead change. Innovative executive education has a critical role to play in delivering such a workforce. To ensure its financial viability and stability, a school offering executive education must have sufficient numbers of students and clients willing to pay for and be a part of what it ultimately produces for the labor market. Globally, there are some 13,000 business schools; and while many of these have adopted efficient models, others have had to restructure or merge in their struggle to survive, and others still have closed their doors.

Due to globalization, technology, demographics, the knowledge economy and the need for environmental sustainability, MBA graduates will need to more effectively manage more volatility, uncertainty, complexity, and ambiguity (the well-known VUCA phenomenon developed from Bennis and Nanus' 1985 strategic management theories) in the coming decade than in recent memory. Today's VUCA phenomena dominating the networked world markets create the need and demand for MBA programs to train and graduate multiculturally skilled, globally intelligent, and adaptive managers. The traditional paradigm of business schools with its focus on analytical models and reductionism is not well suited to fight the ambiguity and rapid, digital transformation changes facing many industries today. Identifying these opportunities into a new model for business schools is vital to educators and policymakers in preparation for seizing upon existing megatrends to create shared value for regional economies in new directions.

Conceptualizing and subsequently testing new models for MBA program is significant to academia and the business sector because today there is more mobility in the workforce than ever before; this is in part due to increased lifespans as well as changes in traditional working conditions, which includes a shift away from lifelong employment in favor of a diverse career portfolio. At the younger end of the workforce spectrum, individuals increasingly expect to be able to vary their career paths and, at the same time, continuously upgrade their skills in the use of new technologies. Organizations and business schools will necessarily have to redesign curricula that cater to the varying attitudes, values, needs, skills, expectations, and aspirations of multiple generations. The changing nature of work is marking international mobility, and driving afresh focus on organizational well-being and work-life balance, and uncertain retirement ages; the management of all these factors will have to be carried out concerning their different contexts and frames of reference. The ability to motivate and lead individuals in this new and challenging reality will unavoidably require new managerial skills.

Today's business schools must strategically engage others in the business and education ecosystems, by a commitment to experimentation and innovation. This is a vision for a future where the MBA curriculum becomes the disruptor to change the narrative about the impact of business education, in society. To educate future executives to transform the coming technological disruptions of industrial revolution 4.0 into an avenue for world economic development and prosperity, MBA program leaders must begin to consider the issue of online technologies in education. Christiansen, Raynor, and McDonald (2015) raised interesting questions as they debated their interpretation of disruptive innovation in higher education in *Harvard Business Review*:

> The *relative* standing of higher-education institutions remains largely unchanged: With few exceptions, the top 20 are still the top 20, and the next 50 are still in that second tier, decade after decade. Because both incumbents and newcomers are seemingly following the same game plan, it is perhaps no surprise that incumbents are able to maintain their positions. What has been missing—until recently—is experimentation with new models that successfully appeal to today's non-consumers of higher education. The question now is whether there is a novel technology or business model that allows new entrants to move upmarket without emulating the incumbents' high costs—that is, to follow a disruptive path. The answer seems to be yes, and the enabling innovation is online learning, which is becoming broadly available. Real tuition for online courses is falling, and accessibility and quality are improving. Innovators are making inroads into the mainstream market at a stunning pace. Will online education disrupt the incumbents' model? And if so, when? In other words, will online education's trajectory of improvement intersect with the needs of the mainstream market? We've come to realize that the steepness of any disruptive trajectory is a function of how quickly the enabling technology improves.
>
> (p. 11)

Applying the theory of disruptive innovation to innovate MBA programs can only be done by developing effective responses to disruptive threats. Failed responses to a disruptive threat are often blamed on a lack of understanding, poor executive attention, or insufficient financial funding. Yet, more needs to be done when higher education fails at being an innovator, such as when a business school may find itself as an entrant who has not sufficiently planned for the future ahead. The innovative business school itself can be seen as a disrupter to further the student experience and to aid the depth of knowledge that a new generation of online business students can achieve through contemporary teaching approaches. The next step in this evolutionary process is for business schools to train their students to transform the coming technological disruptions of industrial revolution 4.0 into an avenue for world economic development and prosperity.

Futurists estimate that up to 49% of jobs could be replaced by machines in the course of the next ten years, while the figure fluctuates for various markets. Toward 2030, there will be an increased demand for software and services that deliver intelligence, personalization, and specialization. AI could become a $15+ billion opportunity by 2025 and double that by 2030. Combining human and machine cognition for engagement decisions could yield the precision and reliability of automation without sacrificing the robustness and flexibility that humans bring. The first effects of industrial revolution 4.0 intelligence will be to lower the cost of goods and services that simply rely on making mankind's life easier, but also more affordable.

Technologies within industrial revolution 4.0 intensify and merge across the digital, physical, and biological worlds; intense shifts are being observed across all industries through the disruption of their incumbents, the development of new business models, and the re-shaping of the systems of consumption, production, transport, and distribution-specific technologies will be significant but the material changes will be to the economic and social systems that form our lives and the way we live. The influence and impact on business schools educating tomorrow's leaders is extensive and all-encompassing. In Figure 3.1 is our co-author Chris Adendorff's construction of complexity of topics for aligning MBA curricula in preparing the leaders who will drive industrial revolution 4.0 over the next decade.

The replacement of jobs by machines has been a continuous trend since the start of the 4IR, but it's anticipated to quicken meaningfully in the coming 10–20 years (Chen, 2017). Certainly, automation can have positive effects, such as on ordinary systems of high-volume processes, where skilled employees are still required to perform complex

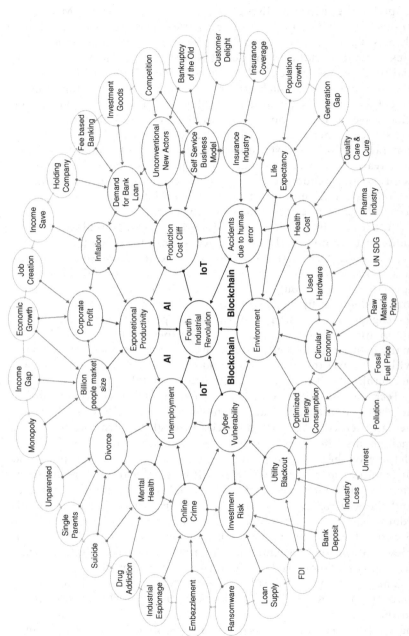

Figure 2.1 Complexity of topics for aligning MBA curricula with industrial resolution 4.0

manual tasks and to manage and control these processes and machines (Adendorff & Putzier, 2018). Consequently, a cumulative number of human–machine interfaces will be established in future industrial manufacturing and production systems (Dombrowski & Wagner, 2014), which will lead to a dramatic evolution in the 'relationships' between man and machine (Leonhard, 2014). While technological revolutions frequently fuel fears of diminishing employment opportunities as "robots do all the work," the elements of the 4IR, being extreme automation and extreme connectivity, may increase the productivity of existing jobs or generate demand for completely new jobs.

Essentially, industrial revolution 4.0 has become the most transformative and disruptive change in history and it is occurring at a rapid pace. One particularly distinctive feature of this era will be the wider application of AI; however, experts the world over are discussing the transformative impact of not only AI, but also technologies such as robotics, 3D printing, and biotechnology, on almost every industry—from manufacturing and retail to healthcare and entertainment—and the massive repercussions for the global economy, as well as the relative competitiveness of developed and emerging nations. New business models, as well as ethical, social, and safety issues, are being encountered as developing technologies come to life.

Industrial revolution 4.0 is a global trend that will result in new ways of creating value, and novel business models will involve increased collaboration between several different partners in international networks of value creation. The full impact on the workforce still needs to be determined, although, according to the World Economic Forum, since 2017 alone digitization boosted global economic output by €142 billion and created 6 million jobs since 2015, and the changes and challenges brought about by digital technologies are certain to continue. Industrial revolution 4.0 cannot be separated from the business school as it mentors its students to tackle with real-world challenges. Business schools are incredible platforms for change in training business leaders to play a direct role in creating economic and social opportunities throughout their regions. Existing and potential talent await to be nurtured and mentored within today's business schools to lead tomorrow's brave, new world.

4 Price-setting models for the innovative business school

Today, price-setting models (PSMs) of business schools are not aligned with student needs. Business schools charge time-based tuition (or licensing/subscription fees). Students invest in education to advance their careers and to increase their salaries to refinance their tuition fees. Future business schools with innovative business models need PSMs to align student needs with their own profitability requirements like, e.g., subscriptions, pay-per-use payment models, or outcome-based performance fees using big data analytics and artificial intelligence. Future business school managers need to understand the opportunities new technologies and pricing strategies offer to be able to charge students for the full value their programs deliver. Innovative business schools over the next decade will use dynamic PSMs to manage cash flow and profitability. PSM innovation is based on the availability of new technologies, and respectively the ability to collect data and to analyze it.

This chapter will start with an educational journey case study before a selection of potential impact factors on pricing decisions of the innovative business school and the need for PSM innovations will be discussed. Based on our theoretical framework, three innovative PSMs are developed for the innovative business school in a student-centered world.

Educational journey case study: Sarah and Tim in a graduate program

Sarah and Tim, two fictitious future students, will accompany us in this chapter to better understand the educational requirements of students in an increasingly student-centered world. Tech-savvy, highly mobile, and with a clear understanding about the value of high-quality education for their future, they expect nothing less than the best. Innovative business schools understand the needs of this highly sophisticated future clientele (including their families) and will use the full potential of new technologies to charge students for the full value their programs deliver. The following educational journey will show potential student needs and how PSM innovations might address them (Table 4.1).

Table 4.1 Case study about price-setting model innovation

Case study—price-setting model (PSM) innovation	Price-setting model (PSM)
Sarah and Tim are looking for a graduate program in digital marketing. On a platform like edX, Ccoursera, getsmarter, or Udacity, they audit several courses of different business schools to understand which program meets their personal needs.	"Freemium"—business schools might use this PSM to attract new students.
Sarah and Tim see that their preferred business schools offer a "nano- or micro-master" in digital marketing. They decide to go for this option before they apply for a full program to better understand the learning outcomes and the requirements. Further, they don't need financial aid to pay for the program and can integrate it in their daily private and professional schedule.	"Buy"—Sarah and Tim pay a tuition fee for the full program.
After successful graduation with a nano- or micro-master in Digital Marketing, they take a "study break" before they apply for a graduate full-time on-campus program in Digital Marketing at the business school where they obtained their nano- or micro-master degree. The business school offers a lean enrollment process and accepts the credits of the "micro-master" as transfer credits for which Sarah and Tim don't have to pay again.	The business school uses a dynamic price-setting tool. Based on the available data about Sarah and Tim, the system calculates their willingness to pay score and sets the basic tuition fee accordingly and offers different payment options: • "Buy"—Sarah and Tim pay the full tuition fee after enrollment. • "RLS"—Sarah and Tim pay monthly tuition fees (all-in flat fee). • "PPU"—Sarah and Tim pay on a credit- or course-based basis.

(Continued)

Case study—price-setting model (PSM) innovation	*Price-setting model (PSM)*
After enrollment, they apply for financial aid to cover tuition fees and other living expenses during their study time.	The business school provides different private and public scholarship and financing options like, e.g., Prodigy finance.
During the program, Sarah and Tim have the possibility to get access to course-based support. Examples are private tutoring (content) or writing center services to boost the performance in a specific course to get a better grade.	"PPU"—Sarah and Tim pay for the service whenever needed.
The business school offers each course on different levels to meet student background, knowledge, and course performance.	"PPU"—Sarah and Tim pay for the service whenever needed.
Sarah and Tim book additional courses whenever needed like, e.g., language courses, leveling courses, career services, company visit, negotiation skills, or study abroad courses at a network partner school.	"PPU"—Sarah and Tim pay for the service whenever needed.
Sarah and Tim identified courses from a network partner school, which they integrate in their personal study plan to make one or more intercultural experiences at business schools in different countries.	The business school purchases this course based on a tuition fee – sharing model (e.g., 50%).
Sarah and Tim worry about getting a job after graduation to pay back their student credits.	Outcome/insurance: The business school offers a partial payback of tuition fees, if they don't get a job six months after graduation.
Sarah and Tim worry whether they are able to meet all graduation requirements within the planned 24 months.	Outcome/guarantee: The business school offers a tuition waiver for six more months to cover the cost risk.
Sarah and Tim have opted for a tuition fee reduction or received a scholarship in compensation for an outcome-based model.	Outcome/bonus: The business school receives a bonus, if Sarah and Tim's salary exceeds a certain level.
Sarah and Tim graduate with honors and end up on the Dean's list.	Outcome/bonus: The business school gives an additional grant as a financial aid to high-performing students.

This case study could easily be continued. As lifelong learners and student/alumni ambassadors, former students like Sarah and Tim remain connected to their alma mater.

Potential impact factors on pricing decisions of business schools

As we have seen in the case study, there are several impact factors, which might motivate a business school to introduce a PSM innovation. Obviously, this short list is by far not exhaustive.

1 Pricing decisions will remain one of the most important decisions of business school managers with the goal to reach a high price-setting power in the sense of the possibility to increase tuition fees without a negative impact on enrollment.

2 We expect a further digitalization of business schools. Thus, decisions makers will have access to more and better data as well as highly sophisticated data analysis tools to assess the willingness to pay of each student leading to individualized, student-centered tuition and service fees based on a combination of the different PSMs.

3 Digitalization requires huge IT investments, which are challenging to finance for most business schools. This will lead to a continuing future growth of EdTech companies or developers of IT platforms for online courses and access to high-quality content like, e.g., Wiley, 2U, Pearson, or edX/Coursera, which offer their services based on tuition revenue share PSMs.

4 Digitalization gives students and human resources (HR) training departments of organizations access to high-quality content and brands for lower cost (tuition and living) (e.g., Harvard Business School Online; edX/MIT; Coursera; getsmarter), predominately in the form of individual online courses and nano-/micro-master programs, which might be integrated in an existing work schedule. Further, it gives students and organizations the flexibility to decide about time, place, and content. This flexibility makes innovative business schools also more interesting for B2B/corporate clients, a client segment that offers a high potential.

5 Digitalization also leads to global pricing, especially for online courses and to an increasing price transparency on price comparison websites leading to a higher price sensitivity of students.

6 Business schools might continue developing the collaboration with other business schools to exchange students and programs. The goal of these networks is to increase the learning experience and outcome for students without further investments. Examples are the possibility to offer dual degrees, to study abroad, or to bring in visiting lecturers for specific contents.

7   Business schools might add different sources of revenue like incubator/accelerator programs to create new businesses together with students, conferences, and publication activities or provide contents and courses for other business schools.

Why do we need PSM innovations?

The goal of PSM innovations is to close the gap between the students' willingness and ability to pay and the actual price (or net cash flow) to maximize the student lifetime value using new methodologies and technologies like big data analytics and artificial intelligence. Besides the actual level and structure of tuition fees, innovative PSMs also cover financial aid and secondary pricing.

Pricing decisions about PSMs intend to increase the price-setting power of a business school. Price-setting power is the ability to increase tuition fees without a negative impact on enrollment, necessary to compensate for cost increases and to charge for added value. The need to gain price-setting power to enforce a price increase of for example 5% annually is existential for every business school to cover growing cost and investments in their competitiveness. Most business schools try to achieve this by adding value to the learning experience to justify price increases. The ability to increase tuition fees by 5% often results in an increase of net profits of 50%, if there is no negative correlation with enrollment.

Theoretical framework for innovative PSMs

We approach our topic "innovative price-setting models" using Figure 4.1. Pricing models or PSMs describe how an organization is monetizing its products and services.

The first pricing decision is the selection of a price-setting strategy. The final goal of each price-setting strategy is to gain price-setting power, i.e., to have the possibility to raise tuition fees without having a negative impact on enrollment. Typical price-setting strategies are skimming, penetration or cost leadership, and differentiation or market-based. Obviously, accreditation, branding, ranking, and other strategic decisions also influence the price-setting strategy of a business school.

The second pricing decision is about the price-setting practice. It is based on the price-setting strategy. We differentiate value-, competition-, and cost-informed practices, which often are used simultaneously to prepare price-setting decisions (Table 4.2).

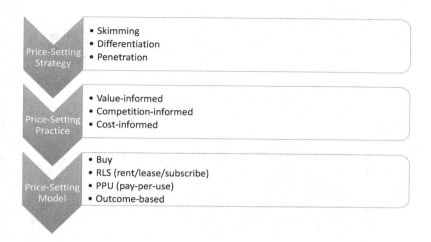

Figure 4.1 Price-setting decisions.

Table 4.2 Theoretical framework of price-setting models

Price-setting model (PSM)	Example
Buy	The student purchases a course textbook and receives ownership.
Rent/lease/subscribe (RLS)	The student pays a time-based subscription fee for a software package and receives the right to use it during this study time.
Pay-per-use (PPU)	The student pays a fee for an additional service like, e.g., private tutorship.
Outcome-based	The student pays tuition fees based on a predefined outcome (e.g., job six months after graduation) or a (partial) payback, if the outcome is not reached. Typical models are insurances or guarantees and income-sharing agreements.

The selection of the PSMs is based on the price-setting strategy and practice. Our theoretical framework uses PSMs. The "buy" PSM describes the situation when a student purchases a course book receiving ownership and generating a single cash flow. In case of a "rent/lease/subscribe (RLS)" PSM, the student purchases a time-based right to access a software package generating recurring cash flows paying a monthly fee. A "pay-per-use (PPU)" PSM charges for

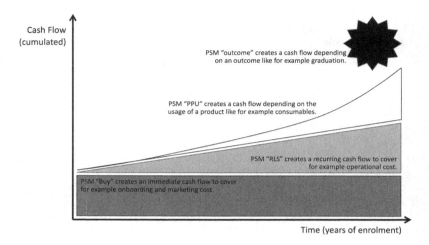

Figure 4.2 Cumulated cash flow using different price-setting models.

the actual usage, generating a cash flow whenever a product or service is used. An outcome-based PSM generates a cash flow, if an outcome is reached or not. Financial aid in the sense of student loans, scholarships, payment plans, or early bird discounts is obviously part of the PSM options of business schools.

Innovative business schools mostly use combinations of all four PSMs as the educational journey of Sarah and Tim has already shown to maximize the value and the cash flow generated by each student (see Figure 4.2).

Innovative PSMs

Based on our assumptions and the theoretical framework, we expect the following three PSM innovations to be adopted by business schools individually or most probably combined. These innovations might integrate several partners on the value chain like competitors/partners (= coopetition), suppliers, and students (Figure 4.3).

Revenue-sharing models

Revenue-sharing models (RSMs) are based on the notion that different firms along the value chain share tuition fees and business risk.

The first example is a <u>tuition fee-sharing model</u> with so-called program management software and content providers (PMSCPs)

Figure 4.3 Price-setting decisions with value-chain partners.

like 2U, Wiley, or Pearson. These PMSCPs offer a software plat-form for online courses including high-quality content and operate basically with a cloud-based software as a service (SaaS) business model. To attract business school clients, they offer a PPU PSM. The business school pays a share of the tuition fee to the PMSCP. Thus, the PMSCP shares the business risk of the business school, because they get only paid, if there is a paying student. Further, the busi-ness school avoids the IT development risk and investment, and IT costs become operational and variable expenses. This is a tempting offer for a business school, but their managers should understand the consequences of such a collaboration as PMSCPs only invest in programs with high student numbers and tuition fees as well as very few change requests. Thus, the business school manager should get well prepared for discussions about program changes with another stakeholder.

The second example is another <u>tuition fee-sharing model</u> where a business school cooperates with another business school (= coopeti-tion model) to offer students an added value of doing a part of their studies at a partner school in another country. An example of such an international business school network is the loosely allied Global Network for Advanced Management (GNAM). It is also a PPU PSM. Besides the intercultural experiences, the credits count to their pro-gram or allow them to earn a dual degree without additional tuition fees, because all involved business schools share the tuition fees for the courses the student is taking at the other business school.

Dynamic pricing

The purpose of a dynamic pricing system is revenue maximization. It is used to better understand the relationship between tuition fees, enrollment, conversion, retention, and cross-, re-, and up-selling rates. Dynamic pricing systems require a fully digitalized business school (internet of things [IoT]) with high-quality data and sophisticated an-alytics to meet their expectations.

Dynamic pricing systems combine all four PSMs (buy, RLS, PPU, and outcome-based) to arrive at a tailor-made and individualized tuition fee and payment plan based on the students' willingness and ability to pay to maximize the student lifetime value and to increase their learning experiences and outcomes. Dynamic pricing might also include the availability of access to financial aid for students with the same goal of maximizing the lifetime value of students. Besides existing tools like scholarships or student loans, new external funding solutions like, e.g., Prodigy Finance (prodigyfinance.com) are available to include in the dynamic pricing system. The innovative business school understands the importance of financial aid to give more potential students access to high-quality education.

The application of dynamic pricing is possible, because business schools offer their degree programs and courses in advance at a fixed start date, with a fixed price, and a fixed curriculum. The problem is that unsold places in a program expire after the course start date leading to a negative impact on profitability. Thus, the only variable, which might be changed, is the price to generate demand and fill the remaining places. Even though capacity is set in advance and can't be modified in an offline course/program, capacity management is much easier in an online program/course. From a strategic viewpoint, an online offer of successful offline and on-campus courses and programs helps to monetize them. In this sense, business schools might face a similar situation as airlines, hotels, or travel tour operators and might benefit from their experiences about dynamic pricing systems. Students and business schools might behave dynamically concerning their decisions about price and purchase. Both can develop beliefs about the future prices and the number of open places. Tuition fees might be changed weekly based on demand using financial aid programs or early bird payment options until the course starts and or all places are filled.

Outcome-based PSMs

Outcome-based PSMs are another possible price-setting innovation to better align the interests of students and universities. Outcome-based PSMs might have the character of an insurance policy, a guarantee, or an income-sharing model (ISM) to reduce the investment risk of students. Besides offering an additional value to students, they might help to increase student satisfaction, retention, and enrollment rates.

- Insurance-type services

  One option of outcome-based PSMs are "insurance" type services to cover or to reduce the investment risk of students. Assuming that every student expects to get a better job with a higher salary after graduation to refinance tuition fees or to payback student loans, a loan payment protection or credit default insurance might cover a part of the tuition fees, if students couldn't find an adequate job several months after graduation.

- Guarantees

  A second option of outcome-based PSMs are guarantees. In contrast to insurance-type services, guarantees have no financial component and don't influence the business schools' cash flow. Examples of guarantees are tuition waivers for one or two additional terms or semesters to allow students to graduate without any additional cost even after the planned study time to protect the students against unexpected and uncovered cost increases.

- Income/profit-sharing model

  The third option is an ISM. The basic concept is that students consider their tuition fees as an investment in their education and as a precondition to make the next career step or to earn a higher salary after graduation. If they are successful, they share a part of their (additional) income to pay their tuition fees. The ISM is an alternative to traditional debt with the goal to align the cost with the value a student receives from the education.

An ISM makes sense for students studying subjects with good job prospects and high expected salaries. The ISM might be financed by students, employers, or investors. In the first case, students share a part of their future income with their alma mater as we have seen in the example of Sarah and Tim. An increasing number of educators like, e.g., Lambda School, Purdue University, and the University of Utah are already testing different versions of ISMs through dedicated funds or collaborating with external partners like, e.g., GS2 (https://incomeshareagreements.org/).

In our second case, the future employer is financing the ISM. In this business model, the innovative business schools teach students specific competences (e.g., actuarial science or econometrics) based on the requirements of employers. If the student is hired after graduation, the employer will pay a share of the income to cover tuition fees, similar to a headhunting fee.

The third case is interesting for business schools offering degrees in entrepreneurship. Students create their own businesses during their studies, probably in an incubator or accelerator owned and managed by a business school. The future innovative business school might hold some shares or own the intellectual property rights of the start-up firm to participate in the development of their value or earning an outcome-based licensing fee.

Conclusion

This chapter has shown that digitalization creates new PSM opportunities for business schools due to better and more available data and analytical tools. The main goal of PSM innovations is to gain price-setting power. This could be achieved by closing the gap between the customers' willingness and ability to pay and the actual tuition fees to maximize the student lifetime value as well as the learning experiences and outcomes for each student.

In a student-centered world, dynamic PSMs allow innovative business schools to create PSMs and payment schemes that meet the needs of each individual student. Future business schools with innovative business models will use this opportunity to design digitalized PSMs to align student needs with their own cash flow and profitability requirements. Therefore, managers of innovative business schools need to digitalize their institution and to know how to use sophisticated data analytics tools to be able to charge students for the full value their programs deliver to give them a unique learning experience.

There is a bright future ahead for Sarah and Tim, because they will get access to a high-quality learning experience to prepare them for their role as future leaders with PSMs that meet their needs, requirements, and expectations in an innovative business school.

5   Internationalization strategies for the innovative business school

Due to increasing globalization, internationalization is highly relevant for business schools. Today, business schools already serve international markets to generate growth using a huge variety of strategies like online platforms, franchising systems, strategic alliances/partnerships, or international acquisitions with more and less success. Innovative business models and technologies or the increasing mobility of students and lecturers offer new strategic alternatives for innovative internationalization strategies, processes, and models to develop new markets earlier, faster, and more efficiently. Business school managers need to be aware of these changes to remain competitive and to fill their next classes.

This chapter will start with a basic understanding about the reasons business schools internationalize and what an international business school looks like. Based on the availability of new technologies and changing student needs, we develop three innovative internationalization strategies for the future business school and discuss in the last section of this chapter how these strategies might be combined.

Internationalization motives

Business schools might have different internationalization motives depending, for example, on their country of origin, their legal status, or on different funding sources. In general, the following four categories of internationalization goals can be distinguished (Figure 5.1):

- Resource- and procurement-oriented internationalization motives are, for example, the access to the best faculty and students or the access to knowledge or funding (e.g., Qatar educational city).
- Sales-oriented internationalization motives include, for example, revenue growth through the enrollment of international students.

Figure 5.1 Internationalization motives of business schools.

- Efficiency-oriented internationalization motives include, for example, geographic risk diversification as well as synergy and scale effects.
- Strategy-oriented internationalization motives are, for example, an international mission or the strategy to increase competitiveness as a research and academic institution.

The internationalization goals of business schools from developed and less developed markets might also be differentiated. Whereas the former might plan to contribute to staff development or to increase revenues through internationalization and to leverage their knowledge and brand on a global level, or to compensate for a reduction in government funding at home (= sales-oriented internationalization goals), business schools from developing markets might be looking for partnerships abroad to increase their home-market competitiveness (= resource- and procurement-oriented internationalization goals).

The internationalization goals of public and private business schools might also be differentiated. Whereas public business schools might welcome additional revenues from international activities (= sales-oriented internationalization goals) to reduce their own cost and faculty from abroad to increase competitiveness (= resource- and procurement-oriented internationalization goals), they might face problems to convince taxpayers to finance new campuses abroad. In contrast to this, private business schools might have more strategic options like, e.g., the development of a global research network (= strategy-oriented internationalization goals), geographic risk diversification and economies of scale of online courses (= efficiency-oriented internationalization goals), or to build-up campus network abroad.

Characterization of an international business school

The "international outlook indicator" of Times Higher Education defines the degree of internationalization based on three criteria: the percentage of students from abroad, the percentage of faculty members from abroad, and the percentage of publications with at least one co-author from abroad. These are important criteria, but an international business school is much more. Internationalization can be described based on abilities to attract the three most important stakeholders, students/alumni, faculty, business partners or based on the academic and research activities of a business school and their place of performance (Figure 5.2):

Figure 5.2 Framework to characterize an international business school.

- Enrollment of international students and development of an international alumni organization (geocentric student enrollment)
- Recruiting of international faculty members (geocentric recruiting)
- Acquisition of international business partnerships (geocentric approach) to get a better understanding about the needs of businesses in different countries
  - Partnerships for career-service purposes (e.g., internships, part-time jobs, summer jobs, and jobs after graduation)
  - Partnerships for practical student consulting projects, life case studies, or corporate programs
- Research:
  - Acquisition of international research funding from government and business partners
  - Publication of research findings in international journals and at international conferences
  - Successful execution of research projects with researchers from business schools from other countries
  - Development of research campuses abroad
- Academic:
  - Design globally standardized programs (e.g., Global MBA)
  - Design locally adapted programs with local content (e.g., Chinese case studies) and in the local language (e.g., Chinese MBA)
  - Establish a global network of campuses to allow students the (online) participation in all programs (e.g., Chinese MBA might be offered on all campuses)
  - Design dual or double degree programs with a partner business school in another country
  - Establish international partnerships with other business schools to exchange students and faculty members

The characterization of the international business schools brings us to the next chapter to develop a better understanding about the design of an appropriate internationalization strategy, which is based on existing competences, to reach the internationalization goals.

Internationalization strategies for the innovative business school

Business schools are very creative in developing strategic opportunities to meet their internationalization goals. They use and adapt most of the existing internationalization strategies depending on their own vision, their resources, and their internationalization goals. Well-established and successfully implemented internationalization strategies are the acquisition of business schools in other countries ("buy-strategy") as the NASDAQ-listed multinational education group Laureate (www. laureate.net) shows or the "build" internationalization strategy of the privately owned EF group (www.ef.com) of the Hult family. Other traditional and widely used "build-strategies" are accreditation-licensing and program-franchising, which give students the possibility to earn a dual or double degree while studying at two different business schools. A famous and successful international joint venture is the China European International Business School (CEIBS) (www.ceibs.edu) between Europe and China.

Due to technological innovations and changing student requirements, new or adaptations of existing internationalization strategies emerged. In this section, we would like to discuss three innovative internationalization strategies for the future business school. This selection is exemplary in order to support business school managers in developing a tailor-made internationalization strategy for their business school.

Global Education Service Exporter

The Global Education Service Exporter internationalization strategy is a low-risk, low resource-consuming internationalization strategy. A business school just enrolls international students in their degree programs without changing anything: content, language, delivery on-campus, instructors. Everything remains the same. This is an aggregation strategy to leverage the existing brand, content, and platforms globally. Even though it is a very successful strategy, numbers were limited due to high cost (e.g., travel and tuition fees) and complicated access (e.g., visas and application procedures).

The rebranding of Harvard Business School (HBS) Online (https://online.hbs.edu) at the beginning of 2019 with the emergence of high-quality online education (e.g., with high completion rates) might be considered as a tipping point. Due to the elimination or reduction of prior limitations, the "Global Education Service Exporter" internationalization strategy experiences an unexpected renaissance while creating a completely new market. We will see, whether this tipping point might be even considered as one of Christensen's disruptive innovations, but already now HBS Online gives a wider audience access to the Harvard brand, quality, experience, and content due to better affordability, accessibility, convenience, and simplicity instead of complication and high cost to join on-campus programs. With this internationalization strategy, the most prestigious business schools can leverage their brand and content globally driven by online education technology.

The "Global Education Service Exporter" internationalization strategy might also be characterized as a "born-global" or "central/single-academic-campus" strategy, especially in combination with the internationalization of unregulated activities. Activities with high market entry barriers are more centralized or globally standardized (e.g., one academic campus due to local accreditation/authorization requirements), whereas activities with low market barriers are more decentralized or localized (e.g., research, alumni organizations, or student acquisition).

It will be interesting to observe whether the initial success of this internationalization strategy will be sustainable or just weaken formerly strong brands, how other business schools and online educational service providers will respond, and what will be the next strategic steps of HBS Online and their competitors. It will be also interesting to observe if one business school will succeed in building such a strong stakeholder network through the use of social media that it will even benefit from a "winner takes it all" effect like we can observe in other industries.

An innovative business school using the Global Education Service Exporter internationalization strategy might also join a Global Business School Alliance without any conflict of interest, which is our second internationalization strategy.

Global Business School Alliances

Another interesting internationalization strategy for the innovative business school is the creation of or participation in Global Business School Alliances. These strategic alliances are voluntary, loosely, contractual collaborations of legally independent business schools with their own brands. Most alliances have just one business school per country to guarantee for a positive balance of coopetition, as the example of the GNAM – Global Network for Advanced Management (https://globalnetwork.io) shows.

Global alliances are created because while business schools have to comply with national (or sometimes even state) regulatory requirements, they need to benefit from global synergies, higher revenues due to international students, and a higher value for students due to global exchange programs and additional programs/courses to remain competitive. Global accreditation and rankings can help to close this gap, but still students highly value public recognition of degrees in their home countries.

Most Global Business School Alliances are quite competitive, because they combine local responsiveness due to their national alliance partners with global standardization in IT, operations, or credit systems. While the different programs remain adapted to national market requirements, scale effects and synergies are realized through sharing of investment risk and aggregation on online course platforms or common administration systems. In these "x alliances", the partners focus on their competitive strengths, like, e.g., an upstream specialist focuses on IT, whereas the downstream specialist on student acquisition. In "Y alliances", the alliance partners focus on sharing experiences and on realizing cost advantages in procurement.

There are many operational advantages of collaboration in a Global Business School Alliance. Well-known examples are the mutual recognition of credits or degrees and increased program consistency, exchange programs for instructors, researchers, and students, research and program development collaborations, common publications and scientific conferences as well as common degree programs and the integration of "top courses" from other alliance partners, and industry partnerships with multinational enterprises.

A "Global Business School Alliance" internationalization strategy in the sense of an "internationalization@ home" strategy is very appealing for public business schools, because they benefit from internationalization through the ability to achieve global scope without mergers and while staying at home as national laws and the public status make international mergers or the set-up of campuses abroad difficult, if not impossible.

Managers of the innovative business school understand that Global Business School Alliances are a strategic option to respond to the future challenges of a student-centered educational environment with individualized content like, e.g., live case studies and research findings from the different regions and countries around the world.

An innovative business school using the "Global Business School Alliance" internationalization strategy might also use a "Global Network Strategy" including wholly owned subsidiaries for research, educational services, or student acquisition, especially in highly attractive markets. This is our third internationalization strategy.

Global Network Strategy

The last strategic option presented in this chapter is called: "Global Network Strategy". This strategy is based on the assumption that stakeholders like, e.g., students, suppliers (e.g., content and program management software providers), and industry partners are often global or part of international organizations. The "Global Network Strategy" is an agile internationalization strategy. The main goal is to respond proactively and flexibly to business opportunities and changes in market attractiveness like, e.g., the regulatory environment.

Follow your students

If an innovative business school has a growing number of students from a specific region, they might dedicate more resources to this market to increase enrollment and retention. One market entry form to implement this option is regional hubs. The students in the different regional hubs might attend lectures on all campuses using online classrooms leading to synergy and scale effects and to a higher number and quality of courses offered. INSEAD Business School applying a regional hub strategy in the form of wholly owned subsidiaries on its three campuses in Fontainebleau (near Paris), Singapore, and Abu Dhabi is a highly successful example for this strategy.

Another indicator for the increasing importance of the Global Network Strategy is the growing care of alumni networks for re-, cross-, and up-selling purposes within a "continuing education" or "lifelong learning" strategy as well as the gaining recommendations for new students. Here, a business school is following their students and their students' networks.

Follow your industry partners

Innovative business schools applying this strategy offer tailor-made education services to key account clients like, e.g., multinational organizations, wherever they are needed, leading to a global satellite or branch campus network. This internationalization strategy might be interesting for private business schools, because companies are increasingly complaining that graduates don't have the required competences and public business schools often lack the strategic flexibility to meet the specific requirements of corporate clients. An industry partner might also be another business school. The innovative business school operates here like an outsourcer by offering individual courses or whole programs to other business schools wherever they are needed.

Follow your suppliers

In other industries, often whole value chains internationalize. Program software management and content providers might motivate their clients (= business schools) within their own internationalization strategy to enter new markets. Due to risk, investment, and revenue sharing, this cooperation might be interesting for both partners.

The success of the "Global Network Strategy" is determined by technology and the ability to use it. Rigid organizational and ownership structures as well as differing national regulation are serious limitations. Growing with stakeholders requires agility, responsiveness, and high stakeholder satisfaction to benefit from the network effect.

Hybrid internationalization strategies

The innovative global business school might pursue one of the strategic options or a hybrid model depending on the attractiveness of the different markets, the market distance (e.g., culture, tuition fees, regulation) (Figure 5.4), and the risk and resource requirements (Figure 5.3).

The backbone of our proposed hybrid internationalization strategy is the "Global Education Service Exporter" strategy. Students from all over the world have the possibility to enroll in online programs and to obtain online degrees (Figure 5.3). In the most attractive markets, the online option will be integrated as an alternative delivery form in the existing programs of the "Global Branch Campus Network" strategy.

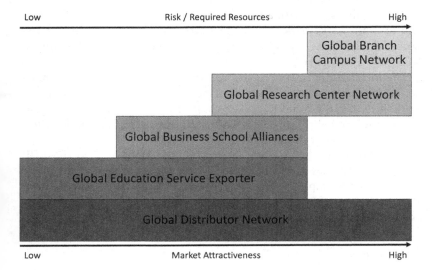

Figure 5.3 Combination of internationalization strategies depending on risk/resources and market attractiveness.

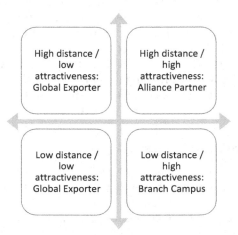

Figure 5.4 Selection of market entry form depending on market distance and market attractiveness.

The second backbone is the "Global Distributor Network" necessary to guarantee the required enrollment rates (Figure 5.3).

In more attractive markets (Figure 5.3) and highly attractive markets with a high market distance (Figure 5.4), the business school might seek a collaboration with a local partner to bridge market differences and to limit market risk. In the most attractive markets with low distance, the business school might opt for a "Global Branch Campus Network" strategy to benefit solely (Figures 5.3 and 5.4).

The internationalization goals and the criteria for the foreign market evaluation and selection of distributor, branch, and research networks (e.g., HBS Global Research Centers) are similar, but different. In an agile and hybrid internationalization strategy, they follow different pathways in varying speed.

The choice of the "right" internationalization strategy is difficult. Often business schools adopt the strategies of leading business schools. For example, INSEAD, HBS, and IE business schools have clear strategies of internationalization that different business schools around the world are expected to replicate.

Conclusions

New technologies and changing stakeholder needs lead to new internationalization strategies. The innovative business school will take full advantage of these new technologies and develop new internationalization strategies based on online delivery and distribution channels (Global Education Service Exporter), their networking coopetition ability with peers (Global Business School Alliances), or following their stakeholders (Global Network Strategy) with changing focus.

Internationalization strategies are used to allow a business school to meet its purpose to produce effective business leaders and to conduct research that has impact on the practice of management. We know that international business education contributes positively to career success and that global organizations need graduates with timely competences to succeed in the workplace and future leaders to solve the growing challenges of mankind globally. Thus, business schools need to internationalize to meet their societal purpose.

It is important to differentiate the internationalization strategies and options of private and public business schools. The latter tend to an "internationalization@home" using Global Education Service Exporter or Global Business School Alliances as internationalization strategies, whereas the former have additional options like a Global Network internationalization strategy with academic, research, and administrative services abroad and might adopt agile and hybrid internationalization models easier.

One further area of interest is the question whether business schools or their service providers like, e.g., accreditation organizations (e.g., The Association to Advance Collegiate Schools of Business (AACSB), Association of MBAs (AMBA), EFMD Quality Improvement System (EQUIS) or program management software firms and content providers (e.g., 2U, Wiley, Pearson, edX, Amazon Educate, Google Classroom) will internationalize faster. Which business model is better internationally scalable, especially from a regulatory perspective? Which business model receives more investments and higher valuations from international investors?

As business schools today channel most of their investments in marketing/sales, accreditation, and digitalization, their original educational purpose, course delivery, might suffer from cost cuts, leaving new strategic opportunities for business models with a higher student and instructor focus. Another interesting question is how social media and online delivery channels lead to a market consolidation or shakeout with the strong brands as "born global" or "winner-takes-it-all" and weaker brands trying to compete with rankings and accreditation labels to build trust and differentiate themselves.

6 The great paradigm shift: business schools leading the global sustainability agenda

In 2015, the United National General Assembly embarked upon a bold vision comprising 17 Sustainable Development Goals (SDGs) focused on several economic, climate change, sustainability, and equality goals for the year 2030. Ranging from goals like no poverty and zero hunger to affordable/clean energy, reduced inequality, and climate action, these goals are meant to encourage dialogue and debate as to how to create a real, better world for its citizens, communities, governments, and relationships in the 21st century.

Although governments and their leaders drafted, agreed to, and will be held accountable for meeting these SDGs, the business world and its leaders will certainly be asked to contribute in meaningful ways—leadership, policy recommendations and implementation, and ongoing good governance—to achieving them, too. As we have clearly seen in our prior research, entrepreneurship—and good business innovation—are keys to reducing poverty. Firms that focus on sustainability—and the so-called "triple bottom line"—are also becoming more recognized as more valuable by both customers and capital markets. Even income inequality, a force in labor markets more substantial than perhaps any shock ever seen, can only be addressed through improved wages, more inclusive leadership, and via better talent management. All of these are directly in the purview of today's modern corporation ... and of its leadership, squarely.

So, what role does the academy play in developing future leaders and managers vis-à-vis these SDGs? How will business schools equip graduates to pursue not only profits but also sustainability of a business's products and services? With respect to climate change, how are young and executive business school participants being challenged to develop strategies that help both a firm's economics *and* a firm's environment? Can leaders trained in best-in-class management practices not only satisfy Wall Street but feed those at the poverty line on Main

Street? Is income inequality just a "not-equals" symbol in a spread-sheet ... or is it a call-to-action for all business executives to address?

Today's business and management schools are ill-equipped, it would seem, to counter such threats and to address such challenges in global (or even local) marketplaces. By definition, business schools today may solve many problems of the past—marketing challenges, capital needs, human resource, and behavior issues, etc.—but may not be that forward-thinking when it comes to some of the challenges mentioned earlier. In hockey-speak, schools are producing graduates who can skate to where the puck is, but, perhaps, not to where it is likely going. Thus, fundamental changes in the ways we teach business students, executives, and scholars are required if business is to play any role—much less a central one—in addressing several of these SDGs in the future. In fact, business schools must get out in front of its graduates—and of its corporate hiring and recruiting partners—and take the leading in setting the global sustainability agenda for the next decade.

What is sustainability, anyway?

The United Nations has defined the following 17 visionary areas (SDGs) for goal attainment by 2030 as part of its "Envision 2030":

1 No poverty
2 Zero hunger
3 Good health and well-being
4 Quality education
5 Gender equality
6 Clean water and sanitation
7 Affordable and clean energy
8 Decent work and economic growth
9 Industry, innovation, and infrastructure
10 Reduced inequality
11 Sustainable cities and communities
12 Responsible production and consumption
13 Climate action
14 Life below water
15 Life on land
16 Peace and justice strong institutions
17 Partnerships to achieve the goal

While all of these areas have some connections to business leaders and to the academies that train them, recent public and private funding, not to mention the attention of Boards of Regents and Overseers, often themselves members of the business elite, have focused on the areas of poverty reduction, (income) inequality, and climate change. Businesses around the world are building entrepreneurial incubators and investment funds to inject capital into ventures that reduce poverty. These ventures create jobs, support public and private assistance to the needy, help build affordable housing, and have been largely responsible for the birth of the microfinance industry as a way to create credit and borrowing—and relatively small levels/scales—to support small, mostly family-owned businesses.

In addition, as the "wealth gap" between the world's richest and poorest citizens widens, business leaders have challenged—and have been challenged—to create more equitable allocations of capital (and of firm ownership, in some cases) to more employees and to the communities in which they operate. Not only will such spreading of this capital hopefully close the gaps between rich and poor but also create communities less starved for investments to fix basic infrastructure and to provide more robust services for citizens. This, in turn, should raise the standards of living—and the minimum wages paid to the most basic of workers—so as to create more "bottom of the pyramid" buying power and economic stimulus. These stimuli can also be used to create more educational and advancement opportunities for the historically disenfranchised so that education levels—and thus service-sector jobs—rise as more and more countries and rural communities depend less on agriculture and more on those economies spurred by the Fourth Industrial Revolution.

But a critical balancing force with such economic advancement is the need to become better stewards of our environment. As heavy (and not-so-heavy) industries have polluted the earth and have depleted its ozone layer, oceans are rising and so are the temperatures around us. Climate change is not only a scientific phenomenon but also a business sector one that must be addressed proactively by business leaders and investors. Creating more jobs on clean energy sources—and less dependence on fossil fuels—is one step. Decreasing carbon "footprints" and emissions is another. But these climate-saving efforts require a workforce that is equal to the task, and this means more training in such skills and services is required. Thus, merely creating training and jobs in these key areas may be possible once, but to create lasting change, such efforts must be sustained over time. Business academies, traditionally focused on current and recent-past best practices, have often been slow to adopt curricula, faculty, and training programs that focus on the talent needed to support such sustainable economic (and business leadership) needs.

Globalization 2.0: sustainability as a business challenge

Sustainability, therefore, is not a concept confined to the policy and development domains. In fact, as the business intersections with society, government, and the environment grow, business schools must see sustainability—and curricula, faculty, and programs that support it—as not just interesting academic conveniences but rather as business imperatives, also. In fact, not only are world markets becoming increasingly dependent on business leadership—and business capital—to help address social responsibility and sustainability needs, students applying to business schools are demanding more training in these areas, too. Governments and corporations—traditional suppliers of students to business academies—are demanding that their managers and leaders become well-versed in how to lead their firms forward not just for shareholder value but also for sustainable environments and businesses.

Leaders, too, want to serve more customer segments—especially those at the "bottom of the pyramid"—who have been historically ignored yet who are, as many Nobel economists have pointed out, quite adept at buying and at becoming brand loyal if they believe a firm sees them as valuable, too. Helping to reduce poverty by providing jobs and good economic value in products and services that cater to these lower-income markets will only create economic stimulus from the bottom-up like those emerging (and huge) middle classes now seen in India and China, for example. But building these business has to be done in ways that maintain a reasonably paid labor force—not via the creation of more "working poor"—and that do not further pollute and damage the earth's natural (and in many cases, non-renewable) resources like water, clean air, and fertile soil.

Therefore, business schools must see sustainable business practices—such as triple-bottom lines, corporate social responsibility, poverty reduction through entrepreneurship, or managing climate change, for both work and environmental "climates"—as new and key focal areas for curriculum reform, faculty research, and community bonding. Not only do sustainable business training programs make good sense in terms of training business leaders to achieve more SDGs, they also make good business sense for business schools who thrive from student tuition and research grant funding. As these two critical sources of revenue for schools become more and more focused on sustainable business practices, climate change, and other SDG areas, so much schools change course and adopt such offerings to its "markets" sooner rather than later. Gone are the days of business schools focusing finance courses on shareholder value, only, or operations courses on raw materials utilization without regard for the environments from where those resources came. More and more students are not only passionate about being taught sustainable business methods and models but are also adversely selecting against those business school programs without any such training listing in their curricular offerings.

Doing well by doing good

Incorporating sustainability goals into business curricula is not simply an evolutionary idea; this is a revolutionary necessity. While some schools have simply added climate change and/or sustainability verbiage to their syllabi, others are truly reinventing their MBA programs, for example ... and the market has taken note. Undergraduate and graduate degree programs are now being rated and ranked based on schools' inclusion of such sustainability principles not just in language but in curricular tracks, faculty hiring, research funding, and community partnerships. For example, accounting courses that do not include "triple bottom line" concepts are quickly becoming the dinosaurs of business degree requirements. Similarly, corporate finance and strategic management courses that do not focus on key community partnerships and "climate KPIs" (key performance indicators) are passé, now, in many degree and executive programs.

As Geoffrey Heal, a Columbia University Graduate School of Business economist, points out, students used to have to make a choice of careers between "doing well" versus "doing good". However, as Heal points out, not only is this choice now a false dichotomy, many students are demanding only careers and jobs where they can both "do well" and "do good" at the same time. This, again, requires transformative curricula, faculty hiring, research foci, and management of student career services never seen before in any prior industrial (r)evolution. Even business schools, themselves, are being urged to practice what they preach when it comes to sustainability goals. Students are demanding fewer printed resources, more sustainable practices from schools and their business partners, and access to potential employers who have, themselves, adopted and demonstrated achievement of at least some level of commitment to key SDGs. Such efforts go far beyond "recycling days" in business school trash collection; these are fundamental shifts in both location and trajectory for most business school programs, today. The "supply side" that business schools offer must now match these leading indicators and needs demand from students, businesses, and society at large if they are to remain relevant—and well-funded—in the future. Lagging programs and schools are already suffering from criticisms of their slow-to-adapt programs, and ironically, some of these, today, are some of the most elite and highest ranked programs in the world.

From producing powerful leaders to empowering stakeholders

In fact, those schools that are lagging in developing focused leadership and management training to support poverty reduction, climate change management, and income equality are, as some scholars have noted, continuing to focus on developing strong leaders devoid of any such skills. This effect may not only create "tone-deaf" leaders in terms of sustainability awareness but may also reduce ever further the power that key community—and global—stakeholders will have in the future of commerce and global markets. Thus, as SDGs become more front-and-center in legislation, society, and academia, business schools and their degree and non-degree programs must move from not just creating power leaders but also having those leaders empower stakeholders in ways not taught before.

University and business school ranking organizations are already focusing on how graduates lead *and* empower employees and staff. However, more ranking organizations are now looking at how these same leaders empower their communities, their governments, and their societies that make up their social ecosystems (both locally and globally). More and more grant applications require specific outputs and proof of community service and partnership, and leaders are asking that business academies train the next generation of graduates to be more in-touch and aligned with stakeholder needs. Simply creating press releases and paying lip service to stakeholders is no longer sufficient; stakeholders now demand as much attention, focus, and investment as shareholders in many respects. This implies that business schools will need to adapt their teaching and learning models to raise awareness to new levels—for new stakeholder groups—like never before.

Marketing leaders will need to better understand impoverished customer segments, and financiers will need to learn to "downscale" their businesses to smaller amounts of capital, consumer loans, and market needs (microfinance). Cross-border community partnerships will also become a norm as more corporations focus on all of the geographies in which they operate, not just the corporate center or country in which they are domiciled. Thus, leaders who lead through policy and process will quickly be replaced by those who lead by empowerment and engagement. Business schools that are slow to adopt these new practices will be training leaders, then, for an industrial revolution that is long past, not the one of the (near-) future.

The big transition: from business training to global stewardship

Therefore, business schools find themselves, today, at a critical inflection point at a time of big transition. Society is no longer asking simply for leaders and managers who can "run the world" but for insightful, connected, and empowering agents and ambassadors who create change in the world, themselves. As more business becomes "boundaryless" and national borders no longer define the rules of commerce, leaders of the future must find ways to become more engaged in "global" affairs—business practices that are global in nature but local in implementation.

The good news is that many of the traditional academic models—systems thinking, for example—will still apply. However, the inputs and constraints on these frameworks have changed. Instead of raw materials, leaders must think of the environmental impacts of investment decisions. Marketers must consider not only product, price, promotion, and placement, but also equality, environment, and engagement. Financial officers will not just think about profits but also about purpose (and, perhaps, the opposite of finance: poverty). Thus, business leaders of the future must engage not just in studying the developing world and world markets but in taking active roles in developing the world, itself. "Financial engineering" may very well transform into "environmental empowerment" while "marketing to profitable segments" may become "managing purposeful services". And the world of talent management will likely shift toward a more balanced view of the future: one in which pay inequality is eradicated and where future leaders worry more about how alike they are with others instead of creating and maintaining gaps and disconnectedness among disparate groups.

However, business schools are only now developing programs to train leaders in these frameworks and techniques and to inculcate them into a culture of sustainability. Without these efforts, business graduates will continue to only react to sustainability challenges, poverty, inequality, and global climate risks instead of taking more control—via collaboration instead of command authority—of the future and shaping it to be better than today's realities and forecasts.

The new currency: paying it forward (vs. paying it back)

But what do incentives look like, then, for business school students. In the past, a business degree was usually a good proxy for increased business success and, therefore, higher income and personal prosperity. However, recent graduates and students today want something beyond significant pay: they want social purpose. They want to work for firms they can identify with in terms of "doing good" and in ways that they feel proud to be affiliated with those firms' social outcomes and results. Emerging business leaders want to focus on the planet before profits and focus on higher purposes than just money. This means, in large part, that future leaders will prefer to lead and to create jobs and opportunities that allow them to "pay it forward" in social terms instead of "pay back" in financial terms. This means that sustainability will not be just an outcome of doing business but a necessary component of any marketing plan to attract talent, investment, and favorable regulatory disposition. Of course, at a curricular level, this means that the traditional marketing curriculum must transform, for example, to one where sustainability—via climate improvement, income equality, and poverty reduction through entrepreneurship—become inputs into messaging and media, not a long-term output that just "sounds good". Students, today, want to make a difference...and they are starting from the outside, in. They are thinking about others, first, and how to make a difference in *their* incomes, livelihoods, and communities.

7 The innovative business school: looking ahead and forecasting trends

Future developments within industrial revolution 4.0 over the next decade entail a high level of complexity and uncertainty, particularly in relation to global economics of scale that indirectly have an impact on business schools. Digital transformation will completely revolutionize the world's governance, trade, and social conditions. It is this factor which makes it possible to liken it to the industrial revolution. It will also do so at an unprecedented pace. Preparedness is key, and therefore, at business schools across the world's regions.

While fossil fuels and their extraction largely fueled growth and development throughout the 20th century, the 21st century has been marked by the expansion of the information and knowledge economies. To this end, it can be argued that big data is the new oil. In the same way that energy policies and access to energy was a determinant of geopolitics throughout the 1800s and into the 1900s, it may be that policies to reformat and protect business schools promote and protect creativity will be the crucial determinants of success in the 21st century (Adendorff & Collier, 2015). If that is true, then educators will have to rethink the way business schools are organized, the way education is planned, the way access to energy and electricity is provided, the way business education is delivered, and the way citizens interact with their communities (Newbigin, 2017). As a result, our fundamental understanding, appreciation, and indeed approach to business education, in all shapes, from scientific to artistic creation, is the defining matter of our time and could not be more important toward 2030 (Bucka & Zechowska, 2011).

The entire social, economic, and political world is being transformed by digital technology. However, this collision with the world of information and communications technology (ICT) and advances in digitalization have constantly forced the discussion of definition for the business schools in relation to industrial revolution 4.0, or better yet, 'digital transformation'. According to the World Economic Forum's Klaus Schwab (2016), who apparently coined the term 4IR, unlike the previous industrial revolutions where humans were liberated from animal power, and mass production was made possible, including early mechanical and digital capabilities, the 4IR is fundamentally different. "It is characterised by a range of new technologies that are fusing the physical, digital and biological worlds, impacting all disciplines, economies and industries, and even challenging ideas about what it means to be human" (Schwab, 2015).

Business schools will therefore need to prepare for impending new technology by establishing an understanding of how it may change society and the global economy over the next coming years; they will furthermore need to decide how to invest in infrastructure and new forms of business education. The following is our forecast of the trends educators should consider in developing their own innovative business school.

Trend No. 1—impact of technology on teaching and learning (how we deliver)

Description: This is a catch-all for everything to do with online learning, digital space, virtual classrooms. Expectations on flexible learning, synchronous/asynchronous. How do we meet this opportunity and challenge? Overseas schools compete in our space then. Artificial intelligence. Virtual reality. Augmented reality. Blockchain.

Trend No. 2—financial pressure on tertiary institutions (our future sustainability)

Description: Increasingly, we will have to paddle our own canoe. How do we ensure we remain fit for purpose, relevant and address our own financial sustainability? Will we remain affordable, value for money? Will we be seen to be legitimate agents of change for the betterment of our stakeholders?

Trend No. 3—academic staff development (will our academics be able to deliver on what we need?)

Description: Transformation imperative, young academics, teaching, research attracting right staff who will meet the future challenges. We are not developing business academics at the rate required. How will we address this? What of insufficient PhDs (for example)? Insufficient black academics.

Trend No. 4—alternative academic offerings (the MBA itself, what is its future? What are the alternatives?)

Description: Is the MBA still worth its salt? Relevant? What does the market need and want? (These are not the same thing). Are we to set the agenda, or to have it imposed on us? Pressure for shorter, specific programs. Applied research? Curriculum design. Our local and global context. Relevant to/in our context. Shaping our own destiny. Maintaining our credibility and standing. What is expected in terms of leadership and management competencies and how we shape/influence these?

Trend No. 5—collaboration dynamics (cross-, inter-, intra-disciplinary)

Description: We can't work alone to make a contribution to solving our challenges. We will have to partner. With whom, how do we set the terms of reference, shape the discourse. How will that impact staffing, structure, skills (etc.) of business schools. This collaboration can extend between business schools, industries, other disciplines (like medical science, biotech, renewable energy, etc., etc.).

Trend No. 6—decline in number of MBA applications due to lack of funding/bursaries for MBA students

Description: Impact on selection decisions.

Trend No. 7—changes in the demographic profile of MBA students in terms of race

Description: Challenge the basic assumptions of established "Western" theories and mindsets. Effects on curriculum development.

Trend No. 8—move from person-centered leadership to contextual leadership

Description: Implications for preparing students for leadership and leadership challenges.

Trend No. 9—increased rate of new entrants

Description: An onslaught of international entrants (with both blended and online offerings) will require schools to differentiate and find ways to provide visible proof points around their offerings.

Trend No. 10—declining government subsidy

Description: Business schools of public universities will need to find other fund-raising avenues to ensure sustainability.

Growing diversification of programs

Trend No. 1—intra-institutional differentiation

Description: Although the market for MBAs will grow, schools will need to invest in offering other programs. Where these conflict with "main campus" offerings, B schools will need to negotiate the degrees they will be allowed to offer relative to other faculties that currently offer M & D degrees in related areas.

Trend No. 2—growing requirement to demonstrate social contribution

Description: Business schools will need to actively decide on the arenas, in which they will make their social contribution.

Trend No. 3—increased government intervention into public universities

Description: The curricula and general discretion of public universities will be increasingly fettered by government. Private universities will be afforded far more latitude and freedom to compete, using business models that will not necessarily include a focus on research.

Education as a service

Trend—changing market demand

Description: More and more global students will be forced to obtain postgraduate qualifications for employment reasons, with specific skills and vocation reasons. This will marginalize the value of qualifications in the long-run.

Public universities will attempt to emulate private business schools

Trend No. 1—competing strategic priorities

Description: Public business schools will be geared toward third income stream activities and short-term goals with quality issues and attempt to emulate trade schools rather than academic schools.

Trend No. 2—employers moving away from traditional business qualifications

Description: The demand of MBA and similar will peak and different offerings will be required. The role of a Doctor of Business Administration (DBA).

Mobility

Trend—integrated education journeys

Description: Students and employers demand that offerings be flexible and integrated with their current workloads.

Transformation of curriculums

Trend No. 1—political expedience

Description: Sound practice and theories will be discarded in favor of politically motivated offerings, without consulting business and employers.

Trend No. 2—changing student/client needs

Description: Time-stressed students operating in an increasingly complex environment, both personally and professionally. This requires diverse delivery options through the use of technology, composition of programs, physical vs virtual delivery variations and styles, with a focus on applied knowledge. Sometimes, deep knowledge and individual competence vs group functionality are required. Thus, less group work is key. Lecturers are to become facilitators of learning rather than mere knowledge transfer agents.

Trend No. 3—*changing business needs*

Description: More and more people specialize in their respective fields and graduate without a strong foundation of the principles of business. Although business needs specialists, there is a greater move toward employing people with general business knowledge and skills. Business requires people who can solve problems in an increasingly complex world and think differently, going beyond a specific area. Business schools need to train people for this.

Trend No. 4—*changing knowledge environment*

Description: More training players disseminating knowledge and focusing on skills, not necessarily formal, have entered the market. Udemy is a good example. They are extremely relevant to business, resulting in some working professionals opting for such training instead of formal qualifications. Similarly, open source learning is emerging more and more, making expensive formal programs questionable. Technology will have a big impact in driving this, where the main driver will no longer be content, but skills or thought processes, where content will only be the vehicle with which the skills are transferred.

Trend No. 5—*technology impact—Fourth Industrial Revolution*

Description: This will also have an impact on the publication of books and articles, where more and more information will become open source.

Trend No. 6—*globalization*

Description: It has become increasingly easier to study business administration internationally, resulting in the competitive environment becoming much larger. Thus, business schools need to ensure that they can give working professionals a globally relevant and competitive experience.

Trend No. 7—*industry-based business school vs university based*

Description: Internationally, there is a move toward business schools to be established and driven by industries or large corporations instead of universities. This has huge implications for business schools not only from a 'teaching' perspective, but it also means that the role of executive training and especially research as we know it will change.

Trend No. 8—growing uncertainty and complexity in the 21st century society

Description: The relevance and value of business education will require constant review and contextualization to assist business and society to make sense of the unknown and the unpredictable.

Trend No. 9—a nagging apprehension about world morality, ethical behavior and trust

Description: Because of previous (Enron) and present (KPMG) unethical business behavior and a sharp decline in the global trust in government and business, the legitimacy and reputation of business and business education per se is expected to come under scrutiny.

Trend No. 10—AI and robotics

Description: The impact of AI and robotics on the workplace is going to force business schools to enhance, innovate, and reform its offerings to suit the requisite competencies and skills of the workplace in the technological era. Critical is their skills of reasoning, analysis, and diagnostic.

Trend No. 11—new entrants with value-adding services

Description: The value proposition of the traditional model of a business school is set to be diluted by the emergence of several other competitors that offer a consulting service to companies as an alternative to business education.

Trend No. 12—socio-economic malaise in the form of poverty, unemployment and inequality

Description: The new role of 4IR trends.

Trend No. 13—stakeholder approach to business

Description: Business schools should produce business leadership intelligence that tackles the triple bottom line and balancing stakeholder and shareholder interests in a globalizing world.

Trend No. 14—digitization & technology disruption of world of business

Description: Exponential increase in digitization is likely to change the business environment dramatically. How will/should this change the curricula of business schools?

Delivery of teaching & technology disruption

Trend—MOOCs

Description: Commoditization of management education via freely available online resources like MOOCs. The drive to move to, or to expect online delivery of teaching— even free online teaching from some international business schools. How will this influence the future of the MBA?

International competition

Trend No. 1—internationalization of the market

Description: Geographical footprint has little impact on the market that can be served. More international business schools are looking to become involved in emerging economies— is this an opportunity or a threat to business schools?

Trend No. 2—sociopolitical instability

Description: E.g., #FeesMustFall, weakening of the exchange rate, inflation, and a lack of government support, can make it almost impossible for business schools to deliver quality MBAs. What about impact from other and other student unrests, and instability in governments due to faction fighting in ruling party, etc.

Trend No. 3—rate of change in business

Description: The dramatic speed of change in the business environment is likely to make it very difficult for business schools to keep up with new and changing business practices.and needs. Increasing distance between what direct clients (the students) value and what the stakeholders (market/rankings/institutions) measure as success.

Digital education

Trend—Fourth Industrial Revolution

Description: The Fourth Industrial Revolution is radically transforming the way in which education is and will be delivered. Students want sophisticated blended education that involves an interactive digitized course and virtual synchronous contact. This requires a shift in an institution's teaching and learning approach, infrastructure, and interaction with students.

Experiential learning

Trend No. 1—workplace-based learning

Description: Workplace learning is becoming increasingly important as this ensures that graduates can transition more swiftly in the workplace. The curriculum should be more practical and applied. Facilitators need to be able to make better connections between theory and practice. More importantly, assessments and discourse should reflect on learnings to encourage deep learning.

Trend No. 2—job placements

Description: International business schools are offering internships and some even guarantee employment with relevant organizations as part of the program. Business schools are required to establish partnerships with businesses so that they can be placed and possibly employed.

Trend No. 3—EduTourism

Description: Countries such as the UK, USA, and Australia are realizing that education can be a lucrative revenue stream for their economy. Business schools will attract students from around the world, which means their curriculum would have to be more globally relevant with an emphasis on global leadership.

Trend No. 4—social and environmental consciousness

Description: A global trend is to be mindful of how our actions impact society and the environment. Business schools need to develop graduates to be more socially and environmentally conscious through dialogues, assessments, and practical projects.

Trend No. 5—*climate change and other sustainability factors*

Description: The imperatives of sustainability are becoming more extreme, including matters of new key performance indicators (KPIs) for business success, ethics, and governance. The uncertainty around the language of sustainability, its misappropriation by self-serving factions, and the emergence of the relational and generative economy make taking decisive business decisions toward positive change for sustainable wellbeing difficult. Preparing future business leaders must include the ability to address these issues. Current low levels of awareness of the subject matter will make it a difficult sell in the contemporary marketplace. It is similarly difficult to attract the few suitably qualified leading-edge thinkers on this topic. Finally, integrating this throughout a full curriculum will be difficult.

Trend No. 6—*advances in data analysis*

Description: The impact of more rigorous ways to model and interpret information (e.g., marketing metrics, qualitative and quantitative data) from electronically mediated and traditional data sources (i.e., the so-called big data).

Trend No. 7—*big data*

Description: New technologies facilitate collecting "big data" and rigorously modeling it to understand complexity, change, and the key drivers of financial, social, and environmental sustainability. The ways that we teach students to understand sources of demand, sources of supply, and methods of effective management must prepare them for this new world.

Trend No. 8—*the mineralization of the research component in the MBA*

Description: Compromises the intellectual output of the MBA by significantly reducing the quantity and range of applied thinking in the degree. No matter that graduated MBAs can theoretically enter PhD study; they simply have nowhere near the grounding to do so. In fact, the MBA is a professional degree, and the Council on Higher Education (CHE) specifications state that they should be able to be admitted to a cognate doctorate—which is a DBA, not a PhD.

Trend No. 9—unbridled digitization of academic programs

Description: Digitization is the new trend that is fast catching up with business schools worldwide. An increasing number of courses are becoming virtual. While this widens access to academic programs to a large number of people and may offer decent revenue for the university, the long-term consequences can be dire, particularly on the quality of academic programs. Digitization may lead to oversupply of business school graduates relative to their demand with ramifications for the job market and the relevance of business school degrees. It may also affect negatively the way learners and teachers interact, effectively shifting face-to-face contact into a virtual world. Lastly, it is my view that digitization will hasten the artificial intelligence world we are in now and cause severe disruptions to student–lecturer relationships.

Trend No. 10—future world of work

Description: In the emerging techno-human society of the 21st century, there are several existential threats to work and jobs as well as shifting employment trends. Many of the roles that business schools are training people for will not exist in the near future, where new skills and competencies will be required.

Trend No. 11—the digitization of courses

Description: There is a need to ensure we are future-facing and evolving along with work trends in order to remain relevant. If we don't, the impact will be that business schools will become redundant.

Trend No. 12—virtualization of education

Description: Less face-to-face student engagement, more online engagement will increase our potential student numbers, while decreasing our overall outgoing costs, provided we keep up with the trend and understand how to scale and scope for this.

Trend No. 13—shifting business models

Description: Failure of consultancy business models like McKinsey, Bain, etc. International collapse of present bureaucratic University business models. Entry of new Universities; Singularity, Apple, Google, Pearson, distance learning important trend, MOOCs, enormous disruptive innovation in teaching, death of University bureaucracies, curricula contested.

Trend No. 14—demand for entrepreneurship

Description: We will need to form entrepreneurial hubs and enter into direct competition with the international consultancies and use our frameworks to attack them. It is from here that we will research and derive our teaching frameworks. It will require new and innovative leadership. The emerging business school leadership types are emerging in the above-mentioned examples.

Trend No. 15—social license of business under pressure

Description: Staying relevant in a business environment, where corporations have a low reputation in helping bridge the economic and social divide.

Trend No. 16—social inclusion

Description: Curriculum and attitudinal changes that provide a more critiqued perspective of corporate and focus specifically at their core on issues of inclusion, informal economy, equity, and exclusionary practices.

Looking to the future and forecasting trends means that the business school of the future—and very much of the near future—must quickly adapt and implement new curricula that do not just include sustainability principles but that are centered on them. Sustainability is no longer an afterthought; it is the leading thought that is requiring programs and graduates to pivot very quickly...or to risk rapid obsolescence.

Keeping it "real"

To be clear, however, the United Nations has articulated its Sustainable Development Goals (SDGs) in the 2030 timeframe; a decade is a long time in academic research, business curricula, and the careers of business school graduates. However, a decade passes faster, now, than ever before. Not only are companies putting leaders on the hook for new and emerging sustainability outcomes but so are governments, societies, and the environment. Such responsibility is certainly awe-inspiring but so are the environmental, sociopolitical, economic, and academic challenges ahead of us. Creating a new generation of responsible and inclusive leaders requires a nearly full retooling of existing business school curricula, faculty research, and career pathing. And this retooling will require more than just a school, its faculty, its research, or its career services organization. In fact, the UN's Goal 17 may sum the need up best: partnerships to achieve goals. Leaders of the future—and the leading business schools of the future—must work in concert with others more now than ever before. This means that stakeholder engagement and empowerment will be critical as will training new managers to affect such change.

The challenges of sustainable environments, income equality, and poverty elimination are too great for any one school to surmount. Thus, partnerships—with other schools, industries, communities, and societies—will become the norm. The "ivory tower" will surely fade into our collective memories as emerging leaders focus more on the planet than profits, more on networks than near-term goals, and more on the environment than on earnings-per-share. But are business academies ready to make the strong pivots required to create this next generation of business leaders? Evidence from students and society's leaders are beginning to show promise, and many of the best practices being proffered in the marketplace are outlined, here, for review and, hopefully, will give way to thoughtful consideration.

Business schools must now operate at the speed of business—perhaps even faster to stay ahead. And while these challenges are not insurmountable, they do require a careful reexamination of how schools teach what they teach, how they get paid for teaching it, and what matters most from their customers. With these insights, the future could be brighter than ever for those schools that embrace evolving business issues like climate change, sustainability, and artificial intelligence. And whatever comes next.

Part 2

The future of the business school

Innovative voices from the field

So what's the next road forward? Business schools must consider a range of megatrends affecting today's business environment when developing innovative training programs for tomorrow's leaders, and as defined by the United Nation's 17 Sustainability Development Goals (SDGs). The SDGs were set in 2015 by the United Nations General Assembly and intended to be achieved by the year 2030, are part of UN Resolution 70/1, the 2030 Agenda. How can business schools mature to mentor tomorrow's leaders in tackling these global challenges?

In this second part of our book we asked to hear from voices across the global business school landscape on what makes for an Innovative Business School. Whether it be new degree programs, research centers, internationalization and collaborative strategies, the embeddedness of AI into business education, creative ideas and new forms of business school faculty and leadership. Of course, this is not to say that these business schools have cornered the market on innovation. What follows in this section are exemplars and hopefully value-added ideas from various countries from which to consider on what can make for an Innovative Business School.

8 The sustainability initiative at IMD Business School, Switzerland

Sameh Abadir, Natalia Olynec and Marta Widz

Founded by business leaders for business leaders, IMD Business School (International Institute for Management Development), based in Lausanne, Switzerland, is an independent academic institution with Swiss roots and global reach (IMD Business School, 2019a). IMD delivers *Real Learning, Real Impact* through a unique combination of teaching, research, coaching and organizational development activities (IMD Business School, 2019a). IMD is the only Swiss business school and one of less than a hundred globally to hold the coveted "triple crown" of accreditations from AACSB, EFMD EQUIS and AMBA, the gold standard for global best practice. IMD has been ranked in the top 5 business schools for executive education worldwide for 15 years, and in the top 3 business schools for the last 8 years in the *Financial Times* rankings (IMD Business School, 2019a).

Integrating sustainability at IMD

Recognizing its responsibility in educating the world's business leaders, IMD has stepped up its action and measurement efforts in the area of sustainability. Buttressing its Sustainability Policy, and sustainability logo highlighting initiatives across campus (refer to Figure 8.1), IMD has integrated responsible leadership in its vision:

> Challenging what is and inspiring what could be, we develop leaders who transform organisations and contribute to society.
>
> (IMD Business School, 2019b)

IMD clearly states in its policy:

> We believe a sense of shared responsibility is essential for the prosperity of individuals, businesses, communities, and nations... We support responsible leaders who act with integrity, contribute to sustainable performance and have a positive impact on the world.
>
> (IMD Business School, 2019b)

IMD sustainability policy, principles, commitment and scope

Source: IMD Business School, 2019b

Our sustainability policy

Founded by business executives for business executives, we are an independent academic institution with Swiss roots and global reach. We strive to be the trusted learning partner of choice for ambitious individuals and organizations worldwide.

We believe a sense of shared responsibility is essential for the prosperity of individuals, businesses, communities and nations. Challenging what is and inspiring what could be, we develop leaders who transform organisations and contribute to society. We support responsible leaders who act with integrity, contribute to sustainable performance and have a positive impact on the world.

Our principles

Our approach to sustainability is aligned with Principles for Responsible Management Education (PRME). PRME seeks to deliver the UN Sustainable Development Goals (SDGs) through responsible management education. We enable continuous improvement to develop a new generation of business leaders capable of managing the complex challenges of the 21st century.

IMD is committed to the following principles:

Purpose

We will develop the capabilities of students and participants to be future generators of sustainable value for business and society, and to work for an inclusive and sustainable global economy.

Values

We will incorporate into our academic activities, curricula, and organizational practices the values of global social responsibility as portrayed in globally recognized initiatives such as the United Nations Global Compact.

Method

We will create educational frameworks, materials, processes and environments that enable effective learning experiences for responsible leadership.

Research

We will engage in conceptual and empirical research that advances our understanding of the role, dynamics, and impact of corporations in the creation of sustainable social, environmental and economic value.

Partnership

We will partner with managers of business corporations to better understand their challenges in meeting social and environmental responsibilities, and to explore jointly effective approaches to meet these challenges.

Dialogue

We will facilitate and support dialogue and debate among educators, students, business, government, consumers, media, civic society and other stakeholders on critical issues related to global social responsibility and sustainability.

We understand that our own organizational practices should serve as example of the values and attitudes we convey to our students.

Our commitment and scope

This policy applies to all IMD programs, events, pedagogic initiatives and research activities. Our impact on the world occurs both directly through our own activities, and indirectly through the activities of the students, business executives and organizations with whom we come into contact.

Figure 8.1 Sustainability @ IMD logo.

With respect to our own activities, our approach to environmental, social and economic responsibility includes working within existing legislation, of course, but also voluntarily exceeding legal requirements to demonstrate leadership on issues that are important to us and our stakeholders. While we have limited influence over the third parties we work with, we commit to educate them about our policy and encourage them to align operating practices with our policy objectives.

In our work with students, business executives and organizations, our goal is to educate effective, inspirational, reflective and responsible leaders who will contribute to enhancing the performance of their organizations in a way that also contributes positively to society. On the research front, we research ambitious and progressive organizations that push the boundaries of performance. We also strive to identify and study individuals and organizations that find innovative ways to do well (performance-wise) by doing good (for society). Beyond our traditional clients and corporate partners, we collaborate with and support non-corporate institutions such as NGOs, NPOs and governmental organizations, to help them manage their activities more effectively and efficiently and thus have an even more positive impact on the world.

Sustainability initiatives at IMD

IMD is an Advanced Signatory of the Principles for Responsible Management Education (PRME), which seeks to deliver the UN Sustainable Development Goals (SDGs) through responsible management education (IMD Business School, 2019b). Its sustainability policy states its commitment to the six principles of: Purpose, Values, Method, Research Partnership and Dialogue. The business school was also granted the EcoVadis Silver Medal rating for CSR performance.

IMD embeds sustainability in its teaching, research, and operations:

Teaching:

- At the heart of IMD's mission is an ambition to encourage and deepen the positive impact that responsible and mindful leaders and businesses can have on society. IMD's CLEAR leadership program, launched in 2018, brings diverse senior executives together to reflect on their roles and responsibilities as leaders. In addition to its other goals, this ten-month program features a unique opportunity to learn from, and help to address, the challenges faced by specific organizations creating social impact in emerging markets. As part of the CLEAR module in Indonesia, business leaders from around the world collaborated in with Kopernik, a social enterprise supporting communities and building partnerships through social innovation in areas such as health, education, agriculture, women's empowerment, and sanitation.

- IMD's flagship MBA program includes a required course on Business and Society led by Knut Haanaes, Visiting Professor of Strategy at IMD and Dean of the Global Leadership Institute at the World Economic Forum. The MBA includes a variety of guest speakers discussing sustainability in business such as Jose Lopez, former EVP and COO at Nestlé, Anne-Wil Dijkstra, executive from Tony's Chocolonely, and Marco Lambertini, Director General of WWF International.

- The MBA also offers a Social Innovation elective by Professor Vanina Farber, focusing on purposeful for-profit business approaches to addressing social and environmental challenges. The course objective is to explore how purpose and sustainability can be the source of innovation of business models.

- For almost 40 years, IMD's MBA Consulting Projects have helped organizations from around the world to assess industry and market challenges, clarify strategic alternatives and act on operational and organizational implications. Companies benefit from research by a team of experienced MBA participants supervised by a dedicated IMD faculty. Several projects have been focused on sustainability issues such as: recycling policies and branding, low-carbon housing, e-mobility, and sustainable logistics.

- Discovery Expeditions: All EMBA participants receive exposure to corporate responsibility issues through Discovery Expeditions that take them to emerging markets such as Peru and Kenya.

Research:

IMD researches progressive organizations that push the boundaries of performance. It also strives to identify and study individuals and organizations that find innovative ways to do well by doing good. IMD regularly develops academic and practice-oriented thought leadership on innovation in the areas of ethics, sustainability and responsible leadership. These include books, practice-oriented research articles, case studies and academic papers.

- "Winning Sustainability Strategies" by Prof. Benoit Leleux and Executive in Residence Jan van der Kaaij is the most recent IMD book on sustainability. It explores the effective design and implementation of sustainability strategies. The book examines practitioner cases from sustainability leaders together with the anonymized results from ten selected industries in the Dow Jones Sustainability Index (DJSI) benchmark.
- Professor Vanina Farber holds the elea Chair for Social Innovation and leads the IMD elea Center for Social Innovation, which inspires and encourages leaders in business, government and civil society to create social innovation, new solutions that benefit global society by addressing social and environmental needs more efficiently and effectively than current policies and businesses. The elea Chair is supported by a donation from the elea Foundation for Ethics in Globalization which was founded by Peter Wuffli, the former Chairman of the Board of IMD.
- The Debiopharm Chair for Family Philanthropy, held by Professor Peter Vogel, facilitates the creation of best practices to strengthen analysis, decision making, evaluation, governance and impact in this area.
- The Kristian Gerhard Jebsen Chair for Responsible Leadership is held by Professor Ben Bryant, who aims to help CEOs transform themselves, their organizations and society.
- The IMD World Competitiveness Center, led by Professor Arturo Bris, publishes the widely recognized annual World Competitiveness Rankings. The center has a unique role in promoting the discussion of socially responsible and sustainable business practices.
- Professor Didier Cossin is the founder and director of the IMD Global Board Center. His research focuses on stewardship, how we can foster organizations to have long-term positive social impact while creating economic value for all.

Access to executive education

Diversity:

- IMD believes incorporating diverse voices is fundamental to understanding how to enable inclusive change in society. The MBA program typically welcomes candidates from 40+ different countries for a class of 90 students. The program "How to thrive as an LGBTQ+ executive or ally" focuses on strategies that drive a more inclusive type of corporate success. IMD also offers programs dedicated to women in business such as "Strategies for Leadership" and places diversity & inclusion in the core content of a broad range of our open and custom programs. In 2018, more than CHF one million was awarded in scholarships of between CHF 10,000 and CHF 85,000 to 34 MBA participants, representing 38% of the MBA class of 90 participants. These scholarships helped attract female students and students from emerging markets.

Not-for-profit collaboration:

- IMD aims to engage more deeply with leaders from the not-for-profit and public sectors to create positive societal impact. For IMD, facilitating access to executive education across sectors is key to building collaboration on solving society's grand challenges. Learning side-by-side with counterparts from the for-profit and not-for-profit sectors create the conditions that push executives to widen their perspectives, identify blind spots, and devise more robust and innovative solutions. Many not-for-profit individuals and organizations would face a financial hurdle to attend IMD programs. IMD welcomes participants from not-for profit organizations in open programs at special rates to engage and develop responsible leaders across sectors. In partnership with not-for-profit platforms IMD aims to bring leaders together from across sectors to create new alliances that foster innovation.

Alumni:

- IMD hosted more than 400 global alumni in 2019 at its Annual International Alumni Event titled "The Future of the Planet–Inspiring What Could Be", devoted to exploring the dilemmas business leaders face related to environmental and social sustainability. The event was part of a campus wide 'Global Goals Week', which highlighted the importance of the action towards fulfilling the UN Sustainable Development Goals.

- IMD regularly supports alumni-founded organizations with social impact:
  - IMD regularly supports GIVEWATTS, a non-profit organization co-founded by IMD MBA alumnus (2008) Jesper Hörnberg. Givewatts brings clean and safe energy to people in developing countries, allowing children to complete their studies.
  - In 2019 IMD's Seasons Greetings campaign supported Hemlata. Founded by EMBA alumna (2016) Smita Grutter, Hemlata funds scholarships, food, medical care, and accommodation, enabling young women in India to attain higher education.
  - The alumni-led Bellerive Impact Fund drives largescale change by pooling resources and skills from the IMD Business School (Switzerland) Alumni Network. It supports entrepreneurs and invests in projects which contribute to achieve the UN SDGs. The Fund aims to prioritize projects which use technology as enabler for their products and services.

The impact of sustainability at IMD is best measured by IMD ability to develop a new generation of business leaders capable of managing the complex challenges of the 21st century.

2019 MBA candidate, Lukasz Kaczynski, reflects on his own journey:

> Sustainability can be an integral part of the business operations, a competitive advantage, not a mere philanthropy or CSR activity. During my MBA, I learnt – for example – how Nestle is contributing to sustainable palm oil production. That was very inspirational. I see myself looking for ways to put sustainability into the core of business decisions in my future career.
>
> IMD engages with more than 9,000 business leaders annually in different degree, open and custom programs. We can have exponential impact by integrating social and environmental considerations in their frame of analysis and decision making," underlined Natalia Olynec, Sustainability Partner at IMD. "It's a great opportunity and responsibility as a leading global business school.

Sustainability in Family Business Award

In its sustainability efforts, IMD is, however, going beyond educating thought leaders, conducting research, and embedding sustainability in its own operations: IMD is also building a community of sustainable businesses and business leaders to inspire others and to set the tone for the future.

As part of this effort, in 2019, IMD and Pictet joined forces to create the IMD-Pictet Sustainability in Family Business Award (SIFBA).

"This special Award has been created to recognize family businesses that have a positive impact on society," explained Sameh Abadir, SIFBA Award Director and Professor of Leadership and Negotiation at IMD. "It was designed to enable, foster, increase, promote and reward sustainable actions and goals" (refer to Figure 8.2).

IMD has a long history of more than 30 years of engagement with family businesses. It was the birthplace of family business education in 1988, when – as one of the first business schools in the world – it started to offer family business programs with the backing of three leaders in the field of family business studies – professors John Davis, Ivan Lansberg and John Ward. In 1989 IMD was one of the founding organizations of the Family Business Network (FBN) and is based in IMD's campus in Lausanne. IMD introduced its flagship Global Family Business Award in 1996 to recognize excellence in family business. IMD was also the first business school to introduce an open program for family offices in 2013.

Family businesses have a unique opportunity to outperform their counterparts in sustainability metrics. "Family businesses understand the importance of long-term thinking, and the impact of what they do or don't do both locally and further afield," stressed IMD President

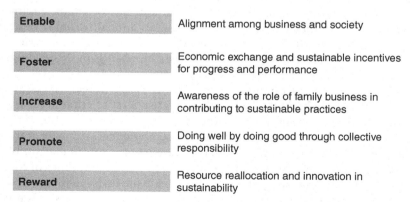

Figure 8.2 IMD-Pictet Sustainability in Family Business Award.

Jean-François Manzoni. "They have a long history of engaging with the communities in which they operate and 'doing well by doing good'."

Indeed, family businesses are said to embody "capitalism with a human face." Next to financial goals, they strive for non-financial goals, cumulatively named nonfinancial utilities, affective endowments, or socioemotional wealth (Berrone, Cruz, & Gomez-Mejia, 2012; Gomez-Mejia, Cruz, Berrone, & De Castro, 2011; Gomez-Mejia, Nunez-Nickel, & Gutierrez, 2001). Socioemotional wealth consists of five distinctive dimensions, as presented in the *FIBER* model: (F) family control and influence, (I) identification of family members with the firm, (B) binding social ties, (E) emotional attachment of family members, and (R) renewal of family bonds through dynastic succession (Berrone, Cruz, & Gomez-Mejia, 2012).

For families in business, the firm 'constitutes a source of family income, security and pride, present and future career opportunities for family members, and a bastion for family reputation in the community' (Le Breton-Miller & Miller, 2008, pp. 43–44). No wonder, family businesses are increasingly prioritizing sustainability.

With the launch of the new Sustainability in Family Business Award in 2019, IMD aims to capture these specific characteristics of family-owned businesses and celebrate those that stand out in their work and commitment towards sustainability.

Inaugural award winner: Firmenich

The inaugural award circle in 2019 included a comprehensive selection process: more than 60 nominations were received from family businesses from across Europe, Asia, the Middle East, North and South America. Eligibility requirements included an annual turnover of at least USD 200 million, international operations, experience in successful succession management, as well as excellence in embedding sustainability throughout the business.

The Evaluation Committee, headed by IMD Research Fellow Marta Widz, analysed the applications against a set of criteria, measuring the breadth, depth, reach, innovation and impact of sustainability initiatives as well as their materiality and alignment with corporate strategy. The committee paid special attention to the role of the family owners in setting the sustainability agenda as well as the ability of the family business to inspire others and advocate for sustainability.

A jury panel of experts, which included – among others – John Elkington, originator of the Triple Bottom Line concept, and Tim Brooks, the Vice President for Environmental Responsibility at LEGO,

Mary Johnstone-Louis, Senior Research Fellow at the University of Oxford's Saïd Business School, Iris Obermueller, Environmental, Health and Safety (EHS) Biopharma Global Healthcare Operations at Ares Trading SA, an affiliate of Merck, Gail Whiteman, Director of the Pentland Centre for Sustainability in Business at Lancaster University, UK, selected Firmenich as the Winner of the 2019 IMD-Pictet Global Family Business Award.

Firmenich – founded in 1895 by Philippe Chuit, Martin Naef, and consolidated in the Firmenich family hands in 1930s – is the world's largest privately held manufacturer of fragrances and flavorings for consumer goods. Its client list includes the world's largest food and beverage, beauty, and household care and fabric companies. The company, present in 100+ markets and operating 82 facilities across the globe, achieved revenues of USD 3.8 billion in 2018 and has more than 7,600 employees.

Firmenich was presented with a trophy, crafted by another family business- Chopard – during the *Family Business: A Voice for Change in Sustainability Forum*, an exclusive gathering of IMD's growing community of family business sustainability champions. The program was a blend of plenary and interactive small group sessions aimed at cross learning among family businesses leaders. The community explored how for many family businesses, sustainability is embedded in their purpose, and also a vehicle to align corporate and family governance as well as engage the next generation.

Sameh Abadir, SIFBA Award Director underlined, "It is the exceptional mix of expertise and the hard work of the team both on the sides of IMD and Pictet that resulted in the phenomenal impact of the co-creation of the award." By bringing together families in business, experts in the sustainability field, leading academics, and jury members, IMD provided a strong platform for networking and exchanging best practices.

9 The MPhil in Futures Studies at University of Stellenbosch, South Africa

Chris Adendorff

Now that as a whole, we have entered the Fourth Industrial Revolution, there is a need to improve the future awareness, or 'future consciousness', of this generation improving its ability to think ahead, to consider, to envision, to model alternative futures, and to respond better to possible, probable, and preferred future eventualities. It was with this mission in mind that the faculty at University of Stellenbosch in South Africa developed the MPhil in Futures Studies, a two-year program to equip future leaders across industry sectors to develop into a professional futurist in understanding local and global issues and their impact on business strategy.

The MPhil in Futures Studies at University of Stellenbosch contributes to learners' ability to make significant strategic long-term decisions in an increasingly internationally competitive and volatile environment. This degree program goes beyond the study of business and future forecasting techniques to also encompass the study of history, philosophy, leadership, sociology, psychology, and industry-specific challenges faced in the Fourth Industrial Revolution. The MPhil in Futures Studies at University of Stellenbosch aims to equip learners with high-level competencies to react meaningfully to growing complexity in the organisational environment within local communities in Africa and South Africa and their unique developmental challenges.

The MPhil in Futures Studies faculty work collaboratively with students to expand the postgraduate learner intake in a field where there is a paucity of expertise. The qualification will contribute to the learners' ability to make significant strategic long-term decisions in an increasingly internationally competitive environment. The program is delivered online over a one-year period, using the delivery platform provided by the Centre for Interactive Telematic Education (CITE), complemented by web-based support. The module methodology is embodied in a series of interactive online lectures and workshops, blended with module material composed of comprehensive module outlines, textbooks, and journal articles. The part-time and online nature of the qualification will allow for a large number of learners to access the qualification, serving South Africa and also beyond its borders. This, in turn, will serve to aid in achieving the objectives of the National Qualifications Framework (NQF) of enhancing the quality of the education and training in South Africa.

We look for achieving these student outcomes:

- Identify, analyse, and understand the theories pertaining to Futures Studies.
- Think critically, logically, and analytically about the systems in Futures Studies.
- Apply strategic management ideology to Futures Studies.
- Select and use a range of research methodologies and techniques to address research in Futures Studies.
- Critique current research and make sound theoretical judgements based on evidence from advanced scholarship in Futures Studies.
- Express an understanding of the leading trends pertaining to Futures Studies.

Critical cross-field outcomes

Upon completion of this qualification, the learners will have acquired specialist knowledge in Futures thinking and be able to apply that knowledge in a critical and problem-solving manner to the problems of the 21st century. Learners will also be equipped to practice as strategic planners within various organisations.

Student are assessed along the following criteria levels to support critical thinking and lifelong learning skills across industry sectors:

Associated assessment criteria of exit level outcome 1:

- Knowledge and application of the formal techniques of evaluating arguments and deductive systems is demonstrated.
- Western philosophers, major movements, issues, and philosophical systems of the early modern and modern era, as well as knowledge of non-western philosophers and philosophical systems, are identified and understood.
- Major philosophical movements and issues in ontology and causality and issues in meaning and theories of knowledge are evaluated.

- The ways in which ethical theory is applied to Futures Studies is discussed.

Associated assessment criteria of exit level outcome 2:

- Critical understanding of the systems thinking philosophy, with a particular emphasis on Futures thinking is demonstrated.
- The ability to use social systems methodology to analyse and understand Futures related issues is expressed.
- Systems thinking is used to define problems and design solutions.
- The use of systems thinking to foster and facilitate organisational development initiatives is illustrated.
- Systems dynamics (causal loop diagrams) are used to develop an understanding of the dynamics underlying systemic problems.

Associated assessment criteria of exit level outcome 3:

- The link between strategic management and Futures thinking/research is evaluated and understood.
- The ability to use Futures Studies to effect change and transformation is demonstrated.
- Resilience theory and the role of leadership within the context of Futures thinking is understood.
- The use of Futures thinking to measure, manage, and mitigate risk is researched and applied.

Associated assessment criteria of exit level outcome 4:

- The use of forecasting techniques to scope the future is demonstrated.
- The use of causal layered analysis to reveal the scope and nature of Futures-related problems and issues is applied.
- Trend and megatrend analysis is used to measure the future.
- Chaos theory, demography, and scenarios are utilised to scope the future.

Associated assessment criteria of exit level outcome 5:

- The history of Futures thinking is evaluated.
- Key concepts of Futures Studies are applied to societal issues.
- A distinction between good and bad work in Futures Studies is identified.
- The use of Futures thinking in a developing country context is analysed and understood.

- Associated assessment criteria of exit level outcome 6:
- The emerging economic, political, social, and technological trends that are shaping the future landscape are identified, analysed, and understood.
- The balancing of economics and technology within ecology is evaluated and understood.

This exciting elective will present many important concepts, theories, methods, and case studies from the future(s) studies field to the students, in such a way that it will expose standards to many new ideas and ways to think about "the future" and their own "preferred futures". Future(s) studies aims to provide the student with insight and understanding of the nature and content of reputable Futures Studies. It outlines the scope, content, and application of future(s) studies in foresight-based planning and management and provides the conceptual methodological basis for Futures Studies as a professional field of multi- and trans-disciplinary academic study.

Our hope is that the MPhil in Futures Studies qualification will contribute towards providing learners with a thorough understanding of the basic principles, history, and philosophy of Futures Studies, by instilling in learners the ability to apply systems thinking to futures-related issues; by enabling learners to identify and analyse the influence of external environmental factors and trends on the future of an entity, and by equipping learners with the ability to use various techniques for measuring future trends. This is what Futures Studies is all about: to develop personal and institutional capability in foresight, idealised futures design and implementation through evaluating attitudes, assumptions, and values, by thinking deeply and systemically about change and future(s) problem solving, by becoming more creative in thinking about the future; and by becoming better in dealing with change through better preparation and application. Even more importantly, Futures Studies have no role within a negative context — i.e., when ideals, values, and beliefs are perceived to be unimportant and our activities and existence on earth perceived to be meaningless. Therefore, although Futures Studies are partly aimed at insight and foresight development, its real value is in its visionary dimension of creating purposeful, meaningful, and sustainable organisations, institutions, and most importantly for our communities that we serve.

10 The MSc in Digital Transformation Management and Leadership at ESCP Europe

Terence Tse

There has been one question at the top of the agendas of many businesses—and parents: how can we better prepare for the future of work? This attention is not unwarrented; new technologies are entering our business lives at a breakneck speed, and while the benefits are welcome, this also significantly affects the current job market. The majority of the jobs the modern education system is preparing its students for will be irrelevant by the time they enter the job market. A couple of years down the line, most will end up in jobs that don't even exist yet. According to the Institute of the Future, as high as 85% of the jobs that today's learners will take on in 2030 are yet to be invented.

However, while there still is significant uncertainty regarding the future workplace and what we should expect, there are some disruptive changes that we cannot ignore.

Some of these key changes that future workers should be mindful of are:

1 The impact of automation and other forms of artificial intelligence on the role of humans in the workplace.
2 The evolution of the "gig economy" and the transformation of the traditional workplace.
3 Increasing importance of soft skills.

There is no denying that the ability to embrace digital transformation and put it to work is becoming ever more important. In a fast-changing marketplace characterised by the drive towards Industry 4.0, digital transformation demands a new way of working and not just new technology. Just as essential as technological know-how is leadership. With this in mind, ESCP Business School launched its MSc in Digital Transformation Management & Leadership. The programme takes a non-traditional approach to business education and focuses on developing the key skills and competencies necessary for the future of work, alongside introducing participants to major frontier technologies and their impact on the economy, society, and business operations.

The MSc in Digital Transformation Management & Leadership is specifically designed to help its students prepare for key roles in the management of business innovation, allowing them to meet the increasingly important yet complex business challenges related to digital transformation and frontier technologies. In order to deliver content that prepares future leaders and executives who are able to manage both people and machines—as well as business and technology staff—the MSc in Digital Transformation Management & Leadership programme was strategically built on four key pillars aimed at future-proofing careers:

Cognitive skills and leadership

Many studies show that the emphasis on technical skills and domain knowledge has lessened over recent years, with soft skills playing a much more prominent role. Therefore, a large part of the programme is focusing on developing the increasingly important skills and competencies required for the future of work in the digital era, where certain human qualities play an increasingly important role. The programme is specifically designed to enable participants to develop skills in the areas of systems thinking and coordination, complex problem-solving, interpersonal communications, personal branding, creativity, emotional intelligence, entrepreneurship, and more.

Skills	Competencies
• Persuasion/negotiation • Attention to detail • Complex problem-solving • Interpersonal communications • Systems thinking/coordination • Active learning • Broad-based knowledge • Personal brand cultivation	• Creativity/originality • Flexibility/entrepreneurial mindset • Emotional intelligence • Fluency of ideas • Perseverance/focused/persistence/tenacity • Social perceptiveness • Contextualised intelligence/recognition, understanding and acting on interconnections and feedback loops in socio-technical settings

Digital technologies

Technology has long become an inseparable part of our lives. In order to be able to hold different roles and careers at the intersection of business and frontier technologies, as well as gain competitive advantage in the digital age, students need to have a holistic understanding of digital technologies and their impact on different business operations and society at large.

The MSc in Digital Transformation Management & Leadership is specifically designed to provide participants with a deep understanding of the business side of frontier technologies such as artificial intelligence, big data, 3D printing, internet of things, social media, blockchain, and robotics, as well as the processes linked to these technologies, including automation, business analytics and others.

Transformation management

Future leader will also need the knowledge and skills to support digital transformation initiatives and develop new thinking and insights into how to lead and thrive in the digital era. The MSc in Digital Transformation Management & Leadership is therefore determined to provide participants with a critical business survival kit by examining the various management tools and techniques in running transformation processes. From Strategy to Change Management, Agility to Project Management, the programme is specifically designed to enable participants with a strategic approach to solving business problems and coming up with new business models as the market evolves.

Professional development

Finally, examinations as a way of assessing knowledge are sadly outdated. This approach is not likely to be the best way for individuals to acquire the competencies needed for our immediate future. After all, soft skills and competencies are not easily measurable and assessable, and examinations are ill-suited for this purpose. With this in mind, the programme has a strong focus on getting students as much practical experience in managing real-life digital transformation projects as possible.

Students benefit from a 12-week guided Company Consultancy Project, a think-tank-format industry research paper instead of a master thesis, a four- to six-month work placement, numerous practical workshops with companies and industry experts, and company visits throughout the year. The MSc in Digital Transformation Management & Leadership is an early example of the shift in the education system that the current environment drastically demands. We, as educators, need to focus on how we can adapt to best help our students prepare for the future.

The future of work will remain at the top of our agendas in the years to come, and we should all be on a quest for continued education and skills acquisition. Be it hard skills such as coding and graphic design or non-tangible ones such as managerial skills and conflict management, keeping a toolbox of know-how that is updated will be the key to staying relevant in this highly competitive market.

11 A gender empowerment initiative at the Enterprise Development Centre of Pan-Atlantic University, Nigeria

Peter Bamkole

The mission of Enterprise Development Centre (EDC) of the Pan-Atlantic University is "To build a network of entrepreneurial leaders through commitment to continuous learning, process improvement and business integrity." In building this network of entrepreneurial leaders, EDC appreciates the role women must play but equally understands that there are inherent constraints that limit women in reaching their full potentials, especially in developing countries. Consequently, EDC has been very deliberate in its approach of helping women cross the many hurdles, break the glass ceiling, and get them to professionally run their businesses and be successful. In more than a decade, EDC has innovatively addressed these challenges that inhibit the growth of women businesses in Nigeria. Three of these programs are being highlighted below:

1 **Goldman Sachs 10,000 Women**—In 2008, EDC became the first of the over 70 institutional partners of Goldman Sachs 10,000 women program to graduate scholars anywhere around the world. Its model was replicated in Liberia and inspired the evolution of the program globally. The philosophy of the program could be broken down into three parts:

   a Build the capacity of the scholars to manage their businesses effectively and efficiently within six months so as to provide a robust knowledge base upon which everything else would be built. Modules taught include Sales and Marketing, Operations Management, Finance and Accounts, Customer Service, Ethics, etc.

   b Provide scholars with value-added services, including mentoring, that reinforce learning, increase confidence, and expose them to the big picture across their various value chains.

Progress was monitored and evaluated over three years in months 6, 12, 18, and 36 while proffering solution to observed problems as they emerged. This allowed for the provision of customized support and ensured that scholars stayed on projected growth trajectory.

c Provide some of the scholars with international exposure and experiences that help them see what others are doing, expand their networks, and help them see where they too can make a difference in their sector, communities, etc.

Key outcome/learning: Goldman Sachs 10,000 women in Nigeria (and around the world) became a network of highly trained women, supporting and inspiring each other to succeed in business. They pointed each other to opportunities and collaborated wherever possible. For instance, if a GS10K scholar is an event planner for a party, be rest assured that she will invite other scholars to bid for the catering, decoration, etc. They understood that they were each other's ambassadors. The program made them to understand that learning is continuous as embedded in our mission statement.

Beyond the growth recorded by majority of the scholars, perhaps the greatest outcome is their understanding that they have been equipped to improve their ecosystem. Femi Olayebi (Cohort 1) of Femi Handbags probably makes the best handbag in Nigeria but today, she is in addition fixing and redefining her entire value chain. In the last three years, she has been running the annual Lagos Leather Fare that brings together all stakeholders in the Leather Industry and together they are now addressing issues around product quality, policies, financing, etc. And with other "entrepreneurial leaders" that have passed through the program, joining forces to making a big impact becomes easier.

2 **Road to Growth (R2G)**— Despite the robust capacity building program, support services, and the significant progress made by these women, one of the challenges noted was that many other women were unable to get unto the program. The available slots were limited and only 450 women benefitted over a five-year period. So, with the World Bank assistance, a blended learning approach was piloted under their "Women X" program, which enabled us double our capacity. A lot was learnt while implementing "Women X", which served as the precursor program for the R2G program that is being sponsored by Cherie Blair Foundation for Women. Over the last three years, R2G has impacted well over 10,000 women, building their capacity through an online learning platform and

this year via an incredible Mobile App—HerVenture developed by "Emerging 360". The focus of R2G is threefold:

a   Build the capacity of women in business, helping them to prepare for growth. A final deliverable on the program is the "Growth Plan". Thus, the women think about their business in the medium to long-term horizon. Up to 90% of the capacity building program were done online. This allows for flexibility needed by the women in balancing their work and family life.

b   To increase women's chances of accessing finance, which is a critical constraint to growth for small businesses in general but more so for women-led businesses. Their learning journey exposes them to various financial institutions and investors, interacting with them and understanding their prerequisite for accessing finance. It also expands their network and provides them with access to what these investors and financial institutions look for.

c   Providing them with networking opportunities not only within R2G but across the entire EDC ecosystem.

The R2G was designed as a "funnel learning system". Everyone who downloads the HerVenture App can go through the course online but without guidance. Then, from this pool, 800 active learners were selected and onboarded onto the R2G program.

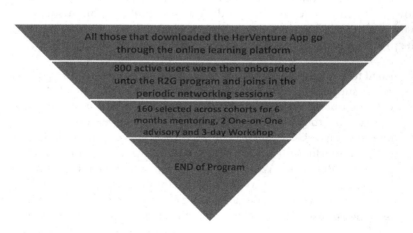

Figure 11.1 Funnel learning system.

These 800 learners were divided into 16 cohorts of 50 each, put in a WhatsApp group and managed by coordinators who are able to track from the backend (of the HerVenture) if they were accessing the app and learning or not. From the answers to the various questions being asked, each coordinator was also able to see where the learners were struggling and with which concept. In order to avoid the "loneliness" associated with online learning, the coordinator passes the tracked understanding of the learners to the facilitator that provides online support throughout the six weeks of learning but more importantly holds a three-hour Zoom class session once a week focusing on the challenging concept(s). If an expert was required for a particular session such as accounting, such expert would be invited. The sessions were recorded and participants have access to these sessions throughout their period of study.

Apart from the scheduled Zoom classes, learners could use the WhatsApp platform anytime to ask questions, clarify anything, or simply contribute to discussions. They could also private chat the facilitator. All of these ensures that everyone was carried along, every voice was heard, and WhatsApp was used as a learning tool. Long after the six weeks, the WhatsApp platform continued to be used by the women in sharing opportunities and experiences. During implementation of their Growth Plans, they used the platform extensively to leverage on peer-to-peer support.

As the women learn, interact, and help each other, they earned points, which contributes to their moving to the next stage of the program where only 160 were then selected. These 160 go through a six-month mentoring program, attend one-on-one advisory sessions and a three-day workshop. This is in addition to the networking meetings they still get to attend that includes master classes on relevant topics.

Key outcomes/learning: Learning becomes a lifestyle and can be done excitingly with mobile phone. Having a trusted peer-to-peer support group strengthens the women and boost their confidence in running their businesses. Sharing experiences on the WhatsApp platform inspires other women to make bold steps especially when free support is available. After the program, a number of them have applied for and received grants through competitions such as the Tony Elumelu Foundation grants ($5,000), the Federal Government Grants (up to $50,000), the Lagos State Employment Trust Fund Loans with subsidized interest rate, the Central Bank of Nigeria's long-term loan without collateral (AgSMES), and a few equity investments. It proves the point that when women are empowered and the right support is provided, the result is a level playing field and they too will excel. The way the program was structured helped in building trust among the women and increased their ability to network. Learning in "bit sizes" enabled the women to make use of every spare time they had and continued wherever they stopped.

3 **Women-in-Tech-Incubator (WITI)**—Having covered the broader constraints that inhibit growth in women-led businesses, it became necessary to look at specific sectors with gender imbalance. While we recognized that this list could be long, we decided to start with Women in technology and tech-enabled businesses because of its cross-cutting impact. With the support of Standard Chartered Bank, WITI program was designed as a one-year, three-tier immersion program with emphasis on active learning and support for the participants.

The learning path starts with a five-month capacity building program, which was reinforced with webinars and business clinics for participants. They also took part in learning labs that exposed them to how others have either birthed their ideas or reinvented their business model. Then, learners progressed to stage two where they were assigned a second year MBA student from the Lagos Business School of the Pan-Atlantic University as a consultant. The MBAs get to practicalize what they have learnt in class and built their capacity to consult while the participants got pro bono quality consulting. They were also assigned mentors at this stage over a period of three months. They were then taken on learning journeys to successful entrepreneurs with systems and structures.

In the last four months of the program, they were then assigned a dedicated coach that helps bring out the best in them so that they could reach their full potential. Corporate governance was introduced at this stage along with its many benefits, especially the assurance it gives to investors. Each participant got a three-man advisory board as part of the process and were part of the monthly breakfast meeting that reviewed the economy and its impact on their various businesses. In a nutshell, participants were handheld over a one-year period on how to structure and run their businesses professionally.

Over the last decade, EDC's focus on gender has been deliberate and strategic. A gender desk has been in existence over the last eight years to ensure that the gender perspective is never missed and in our green building, a free crèche for female learners exist so that nursing

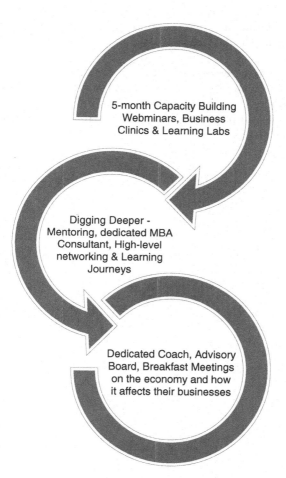

Figure 11.2 Learning path.

mothers can learn as well. Through our programs, EDC continues to align itself with three SDGs.

a Goal # 4 – Quality education: ensure inclusive and equitable education and promote lifelong learning opportunities for all.
b Goal # 5 – Gender equality: achieve gender equality and empower all women and girls.

c   Goal # 8 – Decent work and economic growth: promote sustained, inclusive, and sustainable economic growth, full and productive employment and decent work for all.

If there is a general lesson we have learnt over the decade in addressing these SDGs, it is simply that the process is a marathon not sprint, and commitment must be total with an open mind that embraces innovation that works while quickly discarding methods that doesn't work.

12 An innovative postgraduate Master of Business Administration in Rural Development at University of Allahabad, India

Shefali Nandan

With about two-thirds of total population in India residing in rural areas, rural development assumes greater significance in the Indian context. Rural markets are important drivers of economic growth in India. Though a lot of development of rural areas has taken place and now villages are even connected with modern information and communication technology, yet there are areas that are facing challenges in terms of getting basic facilities like infrastructure facilities and good quality health and education. Many people migrate from rural areas to cities in search of a better life. Holistic rural development involves development not only on economic dimensions but also on social and political dimensions. Various programmes and schemes have been launched and implemented by the Government of India from time to time for improving the quality of life of rural people.

Rural markets hold a huge potential for commercial organisations.

Even non-commercial government and non-government organisations have to cater to the needs of the rural population. Therefore, it becomes important for professionals working in India to know about the rural life of India. In this context, a degree course that facilitates young students to get exposure to rural life and equips them with the required knowledge and skills of functioning in rural areas becomes absolutely essential. It is in this background that the two-year full-time Master of Business Administration-Rural Development, MBA (RD) programme was launched at the GB Pant Social Science Institute, a constituent Institute of the University of Allahabad.

The mission of the MBA-RD programme is to build committed and competent professionals who could transform rural communities by empowering them through enhancement of their awareness levels, decision-making abilities, and management skills, and enabling them to evolve and adopt technologies for sustainable development and adapt to changing demands of the market.

The programme objectives are to train students to become develop-ment managers in the formal and informal sectors of a rural society, develop entrepreneurial abilities, and become change agents. The pro-gramme is designed such that students not only get opportunity for imbibing intensive theoretical knowledge but also get a good exposure to the rural reality. The course develops necessary skills and compe-tencies in the students using various methodologies that include:

Immersion work

Students are inducted in the programme with an orientation session informing them about the institute and the programme. Each student is allotted a teacher-mentor. A two weeks stay in villages is also a part of immersion work with the objective to acquaint students with vil-lages and rural life. They get better understanding of locating bound-aries of a village and identify physical parameters of livelihood and other agro-economic conditions. This also enables them to observe and experience the problems faced by rural people and in general to develop an appreciation of the need for efforts for rural development. Based on the problems identified and needs of the people, a plan for in-itiatives is developed. The visit also aims at helping students to develop qualities that are needed to establish rapport with people/communities and initiate participatory development process.

Course work

There are 27 courses spread over four semesters that include manage-ment courses and rural development courses. Students acquire knowl-edge and skills through an appropriate mix of lectures, field visits, practice, and experiential learning.

Experiential exercises like games, role-plays, simulations, and case studies are designed to help students reflect in a group and acquire requisite managerial and organisational capabilities.

Village work

Village work is undertaken by students in the first two semesters. It provides opportunity to students to live and interact with villagers and understand in depth the rural reality. It aims at sensitizing students to the concerns of rural people and helps them identify the constraints and potentials for development in the area.

Field visits help students relate theory with rural reality. Concepts learnt in the classrooms are used to develop understanding of challenges in rural society. Students go to villages in groups for undertaking task of assessing the needs of local inhabitants in the context of geography, culture, political structure, and existing resources of the area besides ongoing government interventions. Such observations from close quarters develop deep understanding of the issues and practical solutions. They are able to visualise their role as professionals and experience rural living from a change agent's perspective. They record their observations and experiences in field diaries and also formulate research questions. Students prepare field visit reports that enable them to reflect and consolidate their learning. They are required to make a presentation before the final submission of the study report.

Summer training work: training in an organization

A six to eight weeks summer training is arranged for all students with corporate, government, and non-government organisations concerned with rural sector, after the completion of second semester. Summer training is an attempt to bridge the gap between the realities of the professional world and academic learning. It enables students to experience the rigors of professional environment. The training provides a platform to students to be a part of the organisation and learn from actual practice of the skills acquired.

Research project work

Research project, supervised by a core faculty of the institute, is a semester-long project undertaken during the final semester and focuses on in-depth research study on emerging rural issues. The objective of the research project is to provide students with an opportunity to design and create research project independently and apply management insights to complex problems in rural development and management. The research report presentation is done at the end of the semester.

Pedagogy

In addition to classroom teaching and use of reading materials, the programme employs a dynamic approach in teaching learning process.

The following innovative pedagogical methods facilitate in achieving objectives of the programme:

- Reports and documents produced by activist groups and NGOs.
- Folk techniques like folk song, folk dances, etc.
- Experimental and experiential learning exercises.
- Use of reflective methods, learning diaries.
- Interaction with village communities.
- The professionals equipped with MBA (RD) degree get placements in reputed private, government, and non-government organisations that deal/work in rural areas and help in capacity building of rural people and development of rural areas in various ways.

Rural areas, in general, are not a preferred location choice of young people for following a career. Such innovative programmes as MBA (RD) programme enables the youngsters to connect with their roots, understand and feel the actual problems of the rural areas, and propels them into action to alleviate the problems of villagers and improve their quality of life. It motivates youth to work in rural areas and contribute not only to human development but also to economic development of their country.

13 AI and higher education: who is teaching the learners?

Mark Esposito, Terence Tse,
Aurélie Jean and Josh Entsminger

Steve Muyelle, professor and partner at Vlerick Business School, recently wrote: "The Ethically Aligned Design Treatise was created by more than 250 cross-disciplinary thought leaders and includes more than 100 pragmatic recommendations for users, policymakers, and academics who are involved with AI. As the treatise explains:

> As the use and impact of autonomous and intelligent systems (A/IS) become pervasive, we need to establish societal and policy guidelines in order for such systems to remain human-centric, serving humanity's values and ethical principles. These systems have to behave in a way that is beneficial to people beyond reaching functional goals and addressing technical problems. This will allow for an elevated level of trust between people and technology that is needed for its fruitful, pervasive use in our daily lives.
>
> (BizEd Magazine, 2019)

Are we as business school academics ready to teach our students on the ethical boundaries of artificial intelligence (AI) for predicting their and our future by means of human centric and ethical principles and values? This is the next great challenge in the innovative business school of the next decade? In traditional MBA programs, the professor is responsible for the information taught and takes on the responsibility for ethical practices within the classroom. What happens though when the professors do not create the content they teach, but must use a machine's AI algorithms for information to training business leaders of the future? Who is responsible if the information is wrong, or unethical or attempting to control bias in a certain direction? Is the machine or the professor held to account? At a recent TechCrunch Disrupt London conference, Mustafa Suleyman, Google's Deep Mind CEO, addressed this issue by reflecting that "if we don't think consciously as designers and technologists about how we are building those systems, then we will—without realizing it—unwillingly introduce all of those same biases into these systems." It must be up to the educators mentoring present and future business leaders to ensure that the data being processed by AI systems is fair and accurate—similar to a teacher's responsibility to teach with accurate material. So, while educators boldly attempt to embed AI in business school around the world, do we consider what biases we pass on to our students?

Let's take the resurgence of the cottage industry of prediction—serving to help shape what the public should worry about, what they should accept as unlikely, to what they should pay attention. They are the brokers of the modern political imagination. And as we know politics and business have happily coexisted from ancient times. Over recent campaigns, the prediction industry has been increasingly turning to machine learning to drive forecasting. Some, such as MogIA, have been notoriously successful at prediction elections, whereas others, such as Cambridge Analytica, show the power of predicting, or even shaping, political preferences at all. Concern, however, should not simply be with whether the predictions are accurate, but how AI, and all the decisions that can come with its design, reshapes the role of prediction in public discourse.

For as prediction helps to create a divide in the arguments people and pundits use to persuade one another, AI may be appealed to as an additional level of certainty in these points and arguments—a tool to help provide an ostensibly empirical backing to loose judgments and poor representations of uncertainty. Consider the opportunity for Elizabeth Warren, Tulsi Gabbard, or Kamala Harris to take the US presidency. While ostensibly historic for the US, it is hardly a historically new concept; rather, the worry is the opportunity might not be fully captured just by designing a statistically modeling of the same phenomena in relation to the modern trend. Naturally, there are immediate pushbacks to this point— first, such uncertainty depends on what historical data you use to generate the prediction, as there at least 80 countries with histories of female presidents and prime ministers, as well as the record of the popular vote from the 2016 election; second, if you're using historical data without present inputs on the immediate perspective of voters, the prediction will be fundamentally limited in its insights.

Each case points to a need for clearer public representation of the means by which predictions are generated by AI and what this means in the future role of technology in higher education. More fundamentally, it leads to concerns over the design of the machine learning system itself, as designing an algorithm towards statistical trends, such as political or financial prediction, can be fundamentally misleading and distracting. Designing to such statistical trends is not to say that history repeats itself, it is to say we can only reasonably expect history to repeat itself.

So indeed, more often than not, many attempts at prediction tell us more about the people trying to predict than the world they are trying to understand. Prediction tells us how these people, and at some points, the prediction industry at large, see the problem, how they find data, how they ask and frame questions, how they understand what will convince and persuade members of the public. AI systems are extensions of the mental models of the production team, they are expression of their assumptions, their mental models, their biases, as much as the biases of their data.

As such, any appeal to AI systems as a way to provide rigorous validation of political, business, or even public opinions should be met with equally high levels of caution. AI systems are extensions of the mental models of the production team, they are expression of their assumptions, their mental models, their biases, as much as the biases of their data. So, it is not enough to simply acknowledge such mental models, steps need to be made to ensure that cognitive diversity is reflected across the design and use chains—lest AI simply reflect our varieties of ignorance. And isn't education meant to break ignorance?

The world should beware giving credibility to a new divide in the legitimacy of public opinion on the basis of the use of AI—as it can serve to create a wider divide in how people attempt to create opinions at all, and most worrying, in what we believe counts as a persuasive argument. In a world filled with data, it can be easy to conflate data with arguments, trends with the future, historical data for what the world should look like. When used appropriately, AI can be a powerful tool to empower public conversations and strengthen the quality of intellectual debate—but whether such AI systems will be empowering depends on transparency into the design and use of AI, standards for AI's responsible use in media outlets, classrooms, and a better informed public.

The burden of appropriateness needs to fall far before such predictions reach the public stage, with algorithm implementation best practices audit, improved data sampling, synthetic data set usage, nutritional assessment of the data set used—lest AI simply reflect our varieties of ignorance. The collaboration of business schools with computer scientists can mitigate algorithms becoming the surrogates for historical decisions. The growing trend of business schools offering courses from within the liberal arts can continue to hone critical thinking and analysis among its students. Indeed, democracy without the possibility of public persuasion no longer counts as democracy. Each generation rediscovers the past for themselves, and how we use and understand AI in the classroom, just as we see in electoral races, will be a fundamental reflection of the common public consciousness of our time.

So, what do we want future generations to know about us?

14 Not just for business: sustainability curricula at Columbia University

Paul W. Thurman

Columbia University is one of the world's premier universities—consistently ranked in the top ten to twenty universities in the world—and is home to one of the world's preeminent business schools, the Columbia Business School (CBS). In Manhattan, the most densely populated and affluent of New York City's five boroughs, CBS is perfectly positioned to train business leaders of tomorrow at one of the largest finance, consumer products, real estate, and healthcare crossroads on the planet. As the only "Ivy League" university and business school in New York City, students from all over the world compete for coveted admissions slots in order to secure jobs in these disciplines, which are often headquartered merely two to three miles from the Columbia main campus.

Thus, it may come as a surprise that CBS has no part-time MBA program, no distance learning MBA programs, and, perhaps the biggest of all, no MBA track or program dedicated to sustainability, corporate social responsibility, or the environment. Sure, CBS has various (elective) courses in these areas, but the school has chosen to focus on in-person, on-campus learning in the (predominantly) finance and management consulting sectors given its proximity to Wall Street and so many corporate headquarters in the surrounding area. This is not to say that graduates do not pursue careers in other areas—and for certain in those focused on sustainability—but the school does not have a formal degree program in sustainable business, for example.

Instead, Columbia University has a number of graduate-level degree programs in sustainability management, environmental science and policy, climate and society, development practice, and environmental health sciences, just to name a few, sponsored by other (again, top-ranked) graduate schools. For example, the Master of Science (MS) in sustainability management is offered in the School of Professional Studies as is an MS in sustainability science. A Master of Arts (MA) in

Climate and Society is sponsored by the College of Arts and Sciences, a Master of Public Administration (MPA) in environmental science and policy is offered by the School of International and Public Affairs (SIPA), and the Mailman School of Public Health—located on the medical center campus—markets a Master of Public Health (MPH) in environmental health sciences. To see all of these programs in one place, one can go not to the CBS website but to Columbia's Earth Institute resources. A number of full-time and part-time programs—like those mentioned above and others from the School of Engineering, for example—are available to those who are interested.

But again, note that if a search on "sustainability" is attempted on the CBS website, only a few courses offered to MBA students are returned. This is not a criticism but rather an observation that CBS—like many other leading business schools—focus on what has made them successful in the past—and on what has made their hiring firms successful in terms of recruiting graduates—but not necessarily what may lead to greater success (not to mention greater demand) in the *future* of business. (Ironically, in the past, the CBS tag line was something to the effect of, "The Future of Business Starts Here, Today!") So, what does this mean as an example—where we see a world-leading business school neither advertising nor cross-linking its business programs with those sponsored by other schools that focus on sustainability ... if sustainability and United Nations Sustainable Development Goals (SDGs) are front-and-center in business education, today?

Could this mean that CBS is ceding curricular leadership in the sustainability area to other Columbia graduate schools (or to other global business schools)? Certainly not. Most, if not all, of the sustainability programs are cross-disciplinary, and many students desire some exposure to CBS's curricular offerings in this area. Could this mean that other schools are effectively trying to "compete" with CBS to have sustainability-minded graduates enroll in their schools over CBS? Perhaps—recently, admissions have become more competitive in these non-business degree sustainability programs, and applicants who are offered admission to both CBS and non-CBS programs opt to complete their graduate studies in sustainability outside of Columbia's business school. But again, CBS is not asleep at the wheel—the number of environmental, sustainability, and inequity-focused courses, speakers, and research papers coming out of CBS continues to rise in response to both demand ... and supply ... as more researchers and business scholars are interested in the intersections of commerce and sustainability, too.

In addition, Columbia is a relatively large (in terms of graduate programs) university with an endowment that can support multiple schools focusing on a particular research or interdisciplinary area. Other graduate schools with smaller budgets and/or few diverse faculty may try to compete in the "sustainability business" market by collocating such programs inside a faculty of business, economics, political science, or public health. However, the Mailman School of Public Health at Columbia, for example, has created its own focused program on climate and health and has also convened a global consortium on climate and health education to draw both future students and scholars into the field (at both master and doctoral degree levels).

The key takeaway here, thus, is that Universities and, in some cases, the Schools within them, continue to evolve curricula, research, and "clinical care" in the areas of sustainability, climate change, environmental health, and global development. Academic institutions are looking to build sustainability indicatives across departments, breaking the tradition silo mentality of academic departments and schools embedded within universities. An interdisciplinary approach to business education supports MBA students come to grips with sustainable business challenges. Regardless, schools and universities are making progress, and moving forward, more and more cross-departmental programs will be available to students, research scholars, and postdoctoral fellows in these critical and emerging business areas.

15 The Master of Data Science of the Department of Statistics and Actuarial Science at The University of Hong Kong

Olivia Choi

In the era of big data, colossal amount of data is being generated every day from various channels, including social media, retail consumer profile, healthcare, and global economy. The complication of data requires scientists not only to describe and understand the phenomenon but, more importantly, to reveal crucial information to facilitate the best course of action. Given the forthcoming exponential growth and complexity of digital data and in response to the increasing demand for massive data processes, the Department of Statistics and Actuarial Science at The University of Hong Kong, has launched a new taught master program, Master of Data Science (MDASC), jointly with the Department of Computer Science, to teach students how to analyze big data and to enhance the technical skills in formulating data-driven strategies.

In launching an MDASC, The Department of Statistics and Actuarial Science and the Department of Computer Science opened up a new frontier of high-performance analytic center. Data Science is an independent discipline using scientific methods, processes, and systems within the broad areas of statistics, computer science, information science, and mathematics. It aims to examine, translate, and classify data, uncover hidden patterns and unknown correlations, and, most importantly, pinpoint precisely the most critical areas and the implications behind. Data Science helps decipher data and extract valuable information that can be used as strategic part of decision-making. The launch of MDASC provides students an opportunity to acquire the quantitative and analytical skills much needed to stay ahead of the competitive global business environment.

Designated program for individuals

The interdisciplinary approach enhances the applications of computer technology, operational research, statistical modeling, and simulation to decision-making, and problem solving for organizations and enterprises in both private and public sectors. The curriculum of the program adopts a well-balanced and comprehensive pedagogy of both statistical and computational concepts.

The core courses of the MDASC program focus on both predictive and prescriptive concepts and methodologies with an effort to equip students with a solid foundation in statistical and computational analyses. The program is designed for students who were proficient in their fields of study with an undergraduate degree in science, social sciences, engineering, medical sciences, information systems, computer, and data analytics. Students whose interest in high-level analytical skills straddles the disciplinary divide between statistics and computational analytics and wish to pursue further in data science.

Technical skills development

Students are encouraged to learn a broad set of technical skills in the computational and statistical analysis. Computing power has revolutionized the theory and practice of statistical inference. Reciprocally, novel statistical inference procedures are becoming an integral part of data science. The program further reviews the main concepts underpinning classical statistical inference, studies computer intensive methods for conducting statistical inference, and examines important issues concerning modern learning technologies. Machine learning is a fast-growing field in computer science and deep learning is the cutting-edge technology that enables machines to learn from large-scale and complex datasets. Students will be introduced to the fundamental machine learning techniques and then focus on artificial neural networks and learn how to train and optimize machine learning to solve challenging problems.

Data analytics in e-commerce

The second part of the program covers a broad range of contemporary topics and provides students with solid training in diverse and applied techniques used in data science. Multimedia technologies and smart phone apps development are two core courses that enable students to learn how to develop various kinds of media communication, presentation, and manipulation techniques. At the end of the course, students should acquire proper skill set to utilize, integrate, and synchronize different information and data from the media sources for building specific multimedia applications.

The emerging discipline of data science combines statistical methods with computer science to solve problems in applied areas. The program also focuses on how data science can be used to solve business problems, especially in electronic commerce. By its very nature, e-commerce generates large amounts of data, and data mining methods are helpful for managers turning the data into knowledge, which in turn be used to make strategic decisions. The emphasis is developing a core set of principles that embody data science: empirical reasoning, exploratory analysis, and predictive modeling.

Incentive, structured program

Considering the rapid growth of the data science industry, the Master Program normally extends over 1.5 academic years for full-time study, a fast-track completion is possible for special arrangement, subject to approval of the University, and students could choose to graduate in one year. The university believes that no students should be deprived of good education due to financial constraints. To show the commitment to the promotion of equal learning opportunities among students despite different family backgrounds, two scholarships are offered for students entering the MDASC program on the basis of academic merit and admission interview performance.

The Master Program is designed in a practical manner to allow students to solidify their knowledge through implementation. The big data research cluster provides an opportunity for students and the university to widen its leadership and strategies in research, education, and technology transfers in the multidisciplinary filed of big data, and thereby generate bigger impacts to the broader community.

16 The impact of business schools on economic growth in the MENA region

Tricia Bisoux and Sharon Shinn

What impact have business schools had on economic growth in the Middle East and North Africa (MENA)? These questions were on the agenda at The Association to Advance Collegiate Schools of Business (AACSB International) Middle East Summit, held on December 9–10. Nearly 100 administrators and educators gathered in Dubai to determine what they can do to generate the greatest future impact. Although these schools all operate in unique national contexts, they share a common goal: to help their countries thrive by driving innovation, accelerating entrepreneurial activity, and cultivating partnerships that support the exchange of best practices across borders.

"We must form new and stronger alliances with other business schools in the region," writes Thami Ghorfi, president of the ESCA Ecole de Management in Casablanca, Morocco. "Through more joint programs and research projects, we can come together to tackle regional issues and foster knowledge transfer between different countries." MENA countries, says Ghorfi, face three main challenges: unemployment, a weak private sector, and gender inequity. Business schools can help leaders overcome all three. Read more in his commentary, "*Harnessing the Power of Business Education in the Arab World.*"

In 2012, Herb Davis of George Washington University in Washington, D.C., shared with us his experience building capacity of business schools in Iraq. Over the course of the Financial Development Project, backed by the United States Agency for International Development (USAID), several Iraqi universities partnered with schools in the U.S. to improve their programs. Unfortunately, says Davis, by 2014 "most USAID funding for Iraq had pretty much disappeared." Even so, Davis now serves as Distinguished Professor of Business and International Affairs at the University of Dubai's business school, where he continues to work with administrators on private sector involvement. Read more about his experience with the original project in "*Investing in Iraq.*"

Entrepreneurship could well be the primary vehicle to achieve economic growth in MENA countries—an idea that inspired the American University of Cairo in Egypt to launch its Entrepreneurship and Innovation Program three months after the Egyptian Uprising of 2011, when young people marched in protest to draw attention to issues such as inflation, low wages, and high unemployment. "Egypt's youth are passionate, fresh, and experiencing exceptional moments not only in their lives, but in the history of their country," writes Sherif Kamel, then dean and now professor at the AUC School of Business, in his 2012 article "*Entrepreneurial Uprising.*"

"Entrepreneurship will change the lives of Egyptians." By 2013, AUC had launched its Venture Lab (V-Lab) through its Center for Entrepreneurship and Innovation to support even more high-potential startups, an initiative described in "*Ready, Set, Accelerate.*"

Another big source of growth in this part of the world? Small and medium-sized enterprises (SMEs), which the World Bank predicts will drive 60% of employment in emerging economies. This reality is not lost on faculty at the Olayan School of Business (OSB) at the American University of Beirut in Lebanon. "*Scaling Up SMEs*" describes OSB's Growth Readiness Program, an executive education program designed for leaders in this sector. As of mid-2016, the program had helped participants grow revenues by an average 20%.

As the examples above show, change is happening quickly for businesses in the MENA region. For that reason, it's crucial that business schools have access to timely, targeted case studies if they are to prepare the region's future leaders. That's why Tim Mescon, AACSB's executive vice president and chief officer, Europe, the Middle East, and Africa, is especially pleased that The Case Centre has created *The Journal of Business & Management Teaching Cases—Middle East and Africa Edition.* With its first issue slated for June 2020, the journal will "provide local and regional business examples to students enrolled at our member schools in MENA," Mescon writes in a January 16, 2019, blog post.

Business schools in the MENA region are also scaling up access to *education*—and to do that, they'll need a pipeline of talented faculty. In "*Opening Doors for Doctorates,*" we learn about how Brunel Business School in the U.K. and Ahlia University in Hoora, Bahrain, have partnered to create "a PhD without residence." The program allows students—often women—to earn their doctorates as they interact with Brunel faculty via primarily virtual formats. "This home-based model allows our doctoral students in Bahrain to concentrate their research on regional issues that matter to them," writes Zahir Irani, formerly dean of Brunel Business school and currently dean of the Faculty of Management and Law at the University of Bradford in the U.K. "Because most students will not relocate after graduation, their knowledge will stay in the region."

This article was first published as an Editorial blog post in BizEd Magazine.

17 Redesigning business education at European School of Management and Technology: ESMT Berlin

Michael Neubert and Daphne Halkias

ESMT Berlin is a state-accredited Private Business School founded in 2002 by 25 leading German firms. ESMT Berlin is accredited by The Association to Advance Collegiate Schools of Business (AACSB International), Association of MBAs (AMBA), EFMD Quality Improvement System (EQUIS), and Foundation for International Business Administration Accreditation (FIBAA). ESMT is the first business school based in Germany ever to enter the top 10, at number 9 of the *2019 Financial Times European Business School Rankings*. ESMT might be considered as an innovative business school for several reasons, mainly their internationalization strategy and MBA program design. ESMT Berlin's faculty supported by a world-class community of corporate partners offering business students a world-class business education directly linked to solving real-world business problems.

Program design

With their Master degree and Executive Education programs, ESMT offers lifelong learning opportunities for business leaders with a global focus on innovative management, analytics, and technology. Together with the Berlin School of Economics (BSE), ESMT offers a PhD program. ESMT offers four Master's degree programs: Master's in Management, full-time MBA, part-time MBA, and an Executive MBA (EMBA). All ESMT programs benefit from close relationships with ESMT's corporate network and founders, as well as its proximity to the booming entrepreneurial environment in Berlin.

Together with their founding partners, sponsors, and corporate partners, ESMT offers internships and "practice-projects" in the sense of live case studies. Student mentors from the firms give students a real-life experience. "Executives and Entrepreneurs in Residence" specifically enrich the educational programs of ESMT through brown bag lunch sessions, coaching, mock interviews, and career advice sessions, as well as support of wider school events, such as those led by the Investment Club, the Entrepreneurship Club, and the Social Impact Club. The degree programs also offer study abroad programs in international partner institutions.

An innovative feature of ESMT Berlin's program design is the pre- and post-MBA phases as an integral part of a holistic MBA program. The pre-MBA covers optional leveling or make-up courses to get prepared for the MBA program, including topics like German language skills, coding, or quantitative research methods. Further, it offers introductory classes, networking opportunities, and meetings with career services. The post-MBA options include career services, internships, work at incubators or accelerators, fellowships, and research projects with the ESMT faculty. Especially the post-MBA options offer an added value to students, because they give them a useful practical experience for their future career.

Internationalization strategy

ESMT calls itself "Germany's most international business school" based on their international faculty and student body, their global alumni and partner network as well as their participation in international research projects and publications in international journals. ESMT uses a hybrid internationalization strategy.

1   ESMT uses elements of the *Global Education Service Exporter* internationalization strategy. In their academic partnership programs with international business schools (currently in Brazil, China, the USA, and South Korea), ESMT brings their contents through their EMBA degree and executive education certificates to international students all over the world. Further, ESMT enrolls international students.
2   ESMT also applies the *Global Business School Alliance* internationalization strategy. ESMT is part of the international business school alliances UNICON (www.uniconexed.org) and the Global Network for Advanced Management (https://globalnetwork.io) to facilitate the collaboration in academic exchange, research, and student exchange.
3   ESMT operates two campuses in Berlin, Germany and has a branch office in Shanghai, China. It is not really clear whether this single foreign market branch office is the start of a *Global Branch Campus Network* internationalization strategy.

One of the leading drivers for the future of business education will be the emphasis on offering short-term specialized training through certificate programs and partnerships to strengthen business practices within their local business communities. ESMT Berlin's executive education programs and methods is one such example on executive education concentrated on sharing knowledge to impact both the business person's personal development and their company's success. ESMT Berlin is at the forefront of a new trend among completive business schools to offer customized solutions for organizations. ESMT Berlin's executive education programs are designed to equip its students with new approaches, skills, and competencies that are needed to meet current and future challenges. Our hope is that programs within a trendsetter business school such as ESMT Berlin can serve as a benchmark for thousands of smaller business schools worldwide focusing their faculty and students' energies on developing solution pathways for real business problems existing within their communities and beyond their classrooms.

18 International School of Management Paris connects with business beyond its walls

Daphne Halkias and Michael Neubert

The International School of Management (ISM) is a specialized, accredited business school based in Paris, France, with programs on five different continents (Brazil, China, France, South Africa, USA). ISM's mission is to provide business professionals with a strong and knowledgeable foundation in international business to further their careers. ISM Paris provides a program of rigorous academic coursework, support for intellectual contribution, and in-depth exposure to current multicultural business practices.

Candidates come to ISM to master and apply the principles of management in the field of international business. Our focus is on innovation, quality, and institutional leadership in management education. At ISM Paris, we seek way to bring our students closer to a model of learning where education with purpose is central value. We search for ways to connect our students and faculty beyond our walls through building international teaching and research alliances, respecting diversity through practice in our everyday operations and taking our own management programs out to business schools, which are challenged by way of resources and networks. Two of ISM Paris' indicatives to fulfill this purpose are its *External Program Strategy* and the annual *Pitch in Paris Entrepreneurial Networking Event*.

ISM Paris' stakeholders have always considered how they can help other business schools to offer international programs and how they can leverage their competitive advantage of global reach and cross-cultural exposure through an international team of highly qualified lecturers and business schools. The External Program Strategy works on the premise that ISM operates as an outsourcing and offshoring provider of executive education programs for business schools, which are lacking the network or the resources to provide their students with cutting edge and innovative business learning models. ISM Paris is working toward aiding students to receive a double degree from an accredited institution of higher education through participation in its External Program Strategy.

The "Pitch in Paris" is annual entrepreneurial networking event held every December where ISM Paris hosts a business pitch competition. The event is opened to entrepreneurs worldwide and presentations at the actual event can be made in person or through video conferencing, respecting the fact that many novice entrepreneurs with innovative ideas would not have the resources to come to Paris and attend such an event in Paris. The Pitch in Paris focuses on transformative and innovative business models and is an opportunity for hopeful entrepreneurs to get recognized for an innovative business idea, gain valuable feedback, and to network with contacts that could potentially bring their idea to life. ISM Paris' faculty believes this event fulfills one small step in our business with a purpose learning model. Aspiring entrepreneurs in both developed and emerging economies are welcome to seize this opportunity to pitch their business plans to an audience of industry leaders, potential investors, and an influential panel of judges, for the chance to win a cash prize as seed money.

At ISM Paris, our vision is to connect with business beyond ourselves and bring together a diverse community of leaders and learner throughout our impact-generating activities, whose reach will continue to grow each year.

19 The Universidad Paraguayo Alemana: an innovative business school in Latin America

Stijn van der Krogt and Michael Neubert

The Universidad Paraguayo Alemana (UPA) was founded in 2014 by the German private entity SRH, which manages nine Universities of Applied Sciences SRH Group in Germany and by the Union Industrial Paraguaya (UIP) a leading industry association in Paraguay. The University has searched to develop a series of strategies that are to respond to the education and employment challenges of the 21st century.

UPA has developed a teaching and learning process fully based on competence-based learning. This constructivist learning approach translates a four-year learning program that integrates theory, exercises, and project-based learning on a daily basis in a particular academic subject such as mathematics, finance, or production. This is complemented with a transversal subject offered every semester where students are to apply their different acquired competences. This starts with entrepreneurship in the first academic year where students are to set up from scratch their own business venture. The challenges encountered during the business development process generates keen interest in acquiring future knowledge. In the second-year, students undertake an in-company advisory project followed by a project-based internship in Paraguay in the third year and a professional internship in Germany during the fourth year.

The linkage with the UIP enables the University to establish direct and intensive linkages with a network of over 90 private companies and businesspeople in Paraguay and Germany, which provide access to company visits, the integration of live case studies in the curriculum, consultancies, internships and directly generates employment opportunities for graduates. Furthermore, businesspeople directly provide feedback on the competence levels of graduates and additional or new competences the university needs to integrate in its future programs.

UPA responds to the need of the internationalization of education. While internationalization of academic education is widespread in the Eurasian Economic Union (EEU) and Europe, there are found multiple obstacles to generate a more open education system in Latin America. At UPA, internationalization is based on three main strategies. Academic contents are based primarily on academic articles in English. This forces the students to improve their language skills and allows students to become acquainted with up to date learning contents not available in Spanish. The University contracts a mixed team of local and foreign lecturers living in Paraguay and visiting professors, thereby offering students direct access to professionals with different experiences, cultures, and languages. The program also includes a five-month study period at one of the SRH universities and a five-month internship period in Germany. These combined strategies provide a permanent exposure to international trends, people, and experiences contributing to opening up the mental maps of students and lecturers alike.

Finally, UPA pays explicit attention to integrate the latest knowledge of social, environmental, and digital tendencies throughout its study programs. This has resulted in internships and bachelor thesis focusing on topics such as poverty reduction strategies, micro credits, cooperatives, circular and shared economy, industry and agriculture 4.0, creative industries, business intelligence, virtual reality, and blockchain.

Epilogue: "Business schools perhaps need to drink a little more of their own champagne..."

Mark Smith and Federico Pigni

In most languages, there is a phrase like 'the children of cobblers have the worst shoes' or 'doctors don't take their own medicine'. Whichever the phrase, the message is that experts are either too busy or too expert to take their own advice and practice what they preach. Can we say the same about business schools not taking advantage of their own in-house expertise?

Training but which training?

Most research points to the fact that training opportunities are accumulated by those who already have higher levels of education. This both increases educational divides and demonstrates that those who know a lot want to know more. Academics are not excluded from this pattern and invest heavily in constantly learning more about their disciplines and methodologies—it is part of the job! Academics, while always learning more about their particular expertise, spend very little time on formal training beyond it. With the advancement in their careers, academics, like all professional or expert profiles, find themselves playing increasingly managerial-rich roles, for which they may not be trained or sufficiently prepared. The situation may even look paradoxical when management science scholars have in the end to become ... managers! Are they missing a trick?

Investment in management training per se by professionals is a little sparse and sharing their discipline expertise with their closest colleagues rare. Yet, it is not necessarily easy to become a manager of one's peers—not least when one's peers are other academics! As in other professional contexts, it is important for those managing academics to have the space to learn, develop, and reflect on their experiences as managers. A recent European Foundation for Management Development (EFMD) report pointed to the importance of nurturing new higher education leaders and there is a range of training courses available for new deans, new directors of research and emerging programme leaders from organisations such as The Association to Advance Collegiate Schools of Business (AACSB International), EFMD, French Foundation for Management Education (FNEGE), Chartered Association of Business Schools (CABS), etc. However, these programmes are only available for those prepared to go outside their own organisations and perhaps already on a 'leadership track'.

Ready for disruption

The disruptive challenges faced by business schools underline the need for human resource development and leaders prepared to respond and innovate—the arrival of new competition, new technologies, pedagogic innovations, new learning models, and new business models are likely to disrupt further schools conventions around careers and programme formats. Meanwhile, the search for a contribution from business schools to wider society through initiatives such as "Responsible Research in Business and Management" initiative (RRBM) requires academic leaders able to promote change focused on impact and diffusion of relevant research while retaining and developing talent. Indeed, the organisational and commercial challenges for which business schools provide expertise and advice exist inside those self-same business schools. By valorising colleagues through training led by internal experts, business schools could promote access to skill development, share good practice, and promote cohesion between academic and professional support staff.

Time to drink home-grown champagne

As the phrase goes, sometimes 'the solution is under your nose'. Many of our business school academics also have rich experiences as consultants and in world-class organisations, as well as being subject experts. In short, they already bridge the commercial and academic worlds. Likewise, using academic expertise for internal projects reinforces faculty's contribution to their school's development. The scope is huge. For example, academics with discipline expertise can aid the recruitment of professional support staff or can advise on strategy formulation or how to use big data. Meanwhile, the use of collective intelligence can enable schools to identify areas for future development and change.

This diffusion of state-of-the-art good practice can improve the lives of everyone—including managing meetings, time management, effective communication, client satisfaction, diversity, and inclusion. This requires innovative ways to valorise and recognise those sharing and obtaining organisationally relevant competences where, until now, academic competences alone have been valued. Business schools have the tools to respond to the challenges they face today. The expertise is there in our academic departments. The rapidly changing education market means that business schools need to practice a little more of what they preach or as Federico says, "business schools should be drinking their own champagne".

Bibliography

AACSB. (2018). A collective vision for business education. Retrieved May 17, 2018, from https://www.aacsb.edu/publications/researchreports/collective-vision-for-business-education.

Abadir, S., Batsa, E. T., Neubert, M., & Halkias, D. (2019). Leading multicultural teams in agile organizations. Retrieved from *Social Science Research Network*. *ID* 3507635.

Adel, H. M., Zeinhom, G. A., & Mahrous, A. A. (2018). Effective management of an internationalization strategy: A case study on Egyptian–British universities' partnerships. *International Journal of Technology Management & Sustainable Development*, *17*(2), 183–202. doi:10.1386/tmsd.17.2.183_1.

Adendorff, C., & Collier, D. (2015). *An umbrella for the rainbow nation: Possible futures for the Republic of South Africa towards 2055*. Port Elizabeth, SA: CADAR Printers.

Adendorff, C., & Putzier, M. (2018). South African Technology Network International Conference. 4IR, the Role of Universities – "Trends for the Future" – September 11–13, 2018, Durban.

Alajoutsijärvi, K., Juusola, K., & Siltaoja, M. (2015). The legitimacy paradox of business schools: Losing by gaining? *Academy of Management Learning & Education*, *14*(2), 277–291. doi:10.5465/amle.2013.0106.

Alajoutsijärvi, K., Kettunen, K., & Sohlo, S. (2018). Shaking the status quo: Business accreditation and positional competition. *Academy of Management Learning & Education*, *17*(2), 203–225.

Alonso-Martínez, D., Jiménez-Parra, B., González-Álvarez, N., Godos-Díez, J.-L., & Cabeza-García, L. (2019). Taking advantage of students' passion for apps in sustainability and CSR teaching. *Sustainability*, *11*(3), 779. MDPI AG. Retrieved November 20, 2019, from http://dx.doi.org/10.3390/su11030779.

Anderson, L., Ellwood, P., & Coleman, C. (2017). The impactful academic: Relational management education as an intervention for Impact. *British Journal of Management*, *28*(1), 14–28.

Arnett, T. (2014). *Why disruptive innovation matters to education*. Boston, MA: Christensen Institute. Retrieved from https://www.christenseninstitute.org/blog/why-disruptive-innovation-matters-to-education/#sthash.4oUWy4xL.dpuf.

Barber, S. (2018). A truly 'transformative' MBA: Executive education for the fourth industrial revolution. *Journal of Pedagogic Development, 8*(2), 44–55. Retrieved October 31, 2018, from https://www.beds.ac.uk/jpd/volume-8-issue-2.

Barrett, H. (2018a, January 23). *Business schools have a problem with Fintech.* Retrieved September 18, 2018, from https://www.ft.com/content/e336d938-f7ca-11e7-a4c9-bbdefa4f210b.

Barrett, H. (2018b, July 6). *Elite business schools are tone deaf to criticism.* Retrieved September 18, 2018, from https://www.ft.com/content/d4f27022-7e92-11e8-8e67-1e1a0846c475.

Baweja, B., Donovan, P., Haefele, M., Siddiqi, L., & Smiles, S. (2016). *Extreme automation and connectivity: The global, regional, and investment implications of the Fourth Industrial Revolution.* UBS White Paper, World Economic Forum Annual Meeting 2016. Retrieved May 18, 2018, from https://www.ip-watch.org/weblog/wp-content/uploads/2017/09/ubs-vierte-industrielle-revolution-2016-01-21.pdf.

Becker, S. (2018, March 7). *Business schools: Rethink the top-down management model.* Retrieved September 18, 2018, from https://www.ft.com/content/3ad35188-076d-11e8-9e12-af73e8db3c71.

Berrone, P., Cruz, C., & Gomez-Mejia, L. R. (2012). Socioemotional wealth in family firms: Theoretical dimensions, assessment approaches, and agenda for future research. *Family Business Review, 25*(3), 258–279.

Bloem, J., Van Doorn, M., Duivestein, S., Excoffier, D., Maas, R., & Van Ommeren, E. (2014). *The fourth industrial revolution.* Retrieved from Sogeti website: https://www.sogeti.com/globalassets/global/special/sogeti-things3en.pdf.

Bradshaw, D. (Ed). (2017). *Rethinking business education – Fit for the future.* London: Chartered Association of Business Schools.

Broggi, J. D., Duquette, J., Nimura, C., Pattenden, M., Lilly, J., Gallagher, M., San Martín Arbide, L., ... & Winkler, A. (2018). Woolf: Building the first blockchain university. White Paper, Woolf Development Ltd, August 2018. Retrieved October 30, 2018, from https://woolf.university.

Brookings. (2007, February 1). *Top ten global economic challenges: An assessment of global risks and priorities.* Retrieved November 20, 2019, from https://www.brookings.edu/research/top-ten-global-economic-challenges-an-assessment-of-global-risks-and-priorities/.

Brunstein, J., Sambiase, M. F., Kerr, R. B., Brunnquell, C., & Perera, L. C. J. (2019). Sustainability in finance teaching: Evaluating levels of reflection and transformative learning. *Social Responsibility Journal.* doi:10.1108/srj-07-2018-0164.

Bucka, P., & Zechowska, S. W. (2011). The geopolitical determinants of energy security. *Review of the Air Force Academy, 9*(2), 65–77.

Burda, A. (2015). Logistics role in the economy. *Knowledge Horizons. Economics, 7*(1), 170–173. https://ideas.repec.org/a/khe/journl/v7y2015i1p170-173.html.

Çeviker-Çınar, G., Mura, G., & Demirbağ-Kaplan, M. (2017). Design thinking: A new road map in business education. *The Design Journal, 20*(Supp.1), S977–S987. doi:10.1080/14606925.2017.1353042.

Chen, J. (2017). *Future job automation to hit hardest in low wage metropolitan areas like Las Vegas, Orlando and Riverside-San Bernardino.* Retrieved December 11, 2018, from http://www.iseapublish.com/index.php/2017/05/03/future-jobautomation-to-hit-hardest-in-low-wage-metropolitan-areas-like-las-vegas-orlando-and-riverside-sanbernardino/.

Christensen, C. M., & Eyring, H. J. (2011). *The innovative university: Changing the DNA of higher education from the inside out.* Indianapolis, IN: Jossey-Bass.

Christensen, C. M., Raynor, M., & McDonald, R. (2015). What is disruptive innovation? *Harvard Business Review, 93*(12), 44–53. Retrieved October 21, 2018, from https://hbr.org/2015/12/what-is-disruptive-innovation.

Cohen, B., & Neubert, M. (2017, September). Price-setting strategies for product innovations in the medtech industry. In *10th Annual Conference of the EuroMed Academy of Business* (pp. 459–473). Rome, Italy: EuroMed Press.

Cohen, B., & Neubert, M. (2019). The influence of pricing strategies on corporate valuation. *International Journal of Teaching and Case Studies, 10*(2), 125–156. doi:10.1504/IJTCS.2019.101503.

Cornuel, E., & Thomas, H. (2014). Transforming business school futures: Business model innovation and the continued search for academic legitimacy. *Journal of Management Development, 33*(5), guest editorial. Retrieved September 17, 2018, from https://www.emeraldinsight.com/doi/full/10.1108/JMD-02-2014-0016.

Currie, G., Davies, J., & Ferlie, E. (2016). A call for university-based business schools to "lower their walls": Collaborating with other academic departments in pursuit of social value. *Academy of Management Learning & Education, 15*(4), 742–755. doi:10.5465/amle.2015.0279.

Dameron, S., & Durand, T. (2013). Strategies for business schools in a multipolar world. *Education + Training, 55*(4/5), 323–335. doi:10.1108/0040091131 1325983.

Davies, J. (2018). The inner journey of leadership: Preparing leaders for a Vuca world. *Independence, 43*(1), 14.

Davis, H. T. (2012). *Investing in Iraq.* BizEd, May 1. Retrieved November 15, 2019, from https://bized.aacsb.edu/articles/2012/05/investing-in-iraq.

Derbyshire, J. (2019, October 20). Business schools urged to practice what they preach on sustainability goals. Retrieved November 20, 2019, from https://www.ft.com/content/004906f6-e444-11e9-b112-9624ec9edc59.

Dincă, V. M., Ingram, R., Herriot, C., & Pelău, C. (2019). Challenges regarding the internationalisation of universities from Scotland, within the Brexit landscape. *Amfiteatru Economic Journal, 21*(50), 194–208.

Dmitriev, S., Kalinicheva, V., Shadoba, E., Nikonets, O., Pogonysheva, D., & Shvarova, E. (2016). On the impact of innovations on the social structure. *International Journal of Economics and Financial Issues, 6*(1S), 107–113.

Dombrowski, U., & Wagner, T. (2014). Mental strain as field of action in the 4th industrial revolution. *Procedia CIRP, 17*(1), 100–105. doi:10.1016/j.procir.2014.01.077.

Dover, P. A., Manwani, S., & Munn, D. (2018). Creating learning solutions for executive education programs. *The International Journal of Management Education, 16*(1), 80–91.

Dunagan, A. (2017). *College transformed: Five institutions leading the charge in innovation.* Clayton Christensen Institute for Disruptive Innovation, February 22, 2017. Retrieved October 21, 2018, from https://www.christensen institute.org/publications/college-transformed/.

Dunagan, A. (2018a). *Aligning the business model of college with student needs: How WGU is disrupting higher education.* Clayton Christensen Institute for Disruptive Innovation, September 5, 2018. Retrieved October 21, 2018, from https://www.christenseninstitute.org/publications/wgu/.

Dunagan, A. (2018b). *Modernizing the HEA: Congressional priorities for innovation in higher education.* Clayton Christensen Institute for Disruptive Innovation, January 23, 2018. Retrieved October 21, 2018, from https://www.christenseninstitute.org/publications/hea/.

Dyllick, T. (2015). Responsible management education for a sustainable world: The challenges for business schools. *Journal of Management Development, 34*(1), 16–33. doi:10.1108/JMD-02-2013-0022.

Edgecliffe-Johnson, A. (2019, October 20). *Are academics lagging in debate on the future of business?* Retrieved November 20, 2019, from https://www.ft.com/content/00c9006c-e445-11e9-b112-9624ec9edc59.

Elkin, G., Devjee, F., & Farnsworth, J. (2005). Visualising the "internationalisation" of universities. *International Journal of Educational Management, 19*(4), 318–329. doi:10.1108/09513540510599644.

Esposito, M. (2019). Perspective – The future of government: Navigating legislation in the sharing economy. *Future governments (actions and insights – Middle East North Africa, Vol. 7).* Bingley, UK: Emerald Publishing Limited, pp. 327–346. doi:10.1108/S2048-757620190000007018.

Esposito, M., Tse, T., & Soufani, K. (2018). Introducing a circular economy: New thinking with new managerial and policy implications. *California Management Review, 60*(3), 5–19.

Estelami, H. (2017). The pedagogical and institutional impact of disruptive innovations in distance business education. *American Journal of Business Education, 10*(3), 97–108.

Faivre-Tavignot, B. (2019, April 17). *Making a change: Teaching sustainable and inclusive business.* Retrieved November 20, 2019, from https://www.hec.edu/en/knowledge/articles/making-change-teaching-sustainable-and-inclusive-business#.

Falcioni, J. G. (2016). Mastering the fourth industrial revolution. *Mechanical Engineering, 138*(3), 6.

Falkenstein, M. (2018). *Business schools need to reconnect with society.* University World News, June 22, 2018, 4 p. Retrieved September 17, 2018, from http://www.universityworldnews.com/article.php?story=2018061914274232.

Ghorfi, T. (2016). *Harnessing the power of business education in the Arab world.* BizEd, June 1. Retrieved November 14, 2019, from https://bized.aacsb.edu/articles/2016/06/harnessing-business-education-in-arab-world.

Girdzijauskaite, E., Radzeviciene, A., Jakubavicius, A., & Banaitis, A. (2019). International branch campuses as an entry mode to the foreign education market. *Administrative Sciences, 9*(2), 44. doi:10.3390/admsci9020044.

Glen, R., Suciu, C., & Baughn, C. (2014). The need for design thinking in business schools – A review. *Academy of Management Learning & Education*, *13*(4), 653–667. doi:10.5465/amle.2012.0308.

Gomez-Mejia, L. R., Cruz, C., Berrone, P., & De Castro, J. (2011). The bind that ties: Socioemotional wealth preservation in family firms. *The Academy of Management Annals*, *5*(1), 653–707.

Gomez-Mejia, L. R., Nunez-Nickel, M., & Gutierrez, I. (2001). The role of family ties in agency contracts. *Academy of Management Journal*, *44*(1), 81–95.

Gousgounis, Y. Y. L., & Neubert, M. (2019). Price-setting strategies and practice for medical devices used by consumers. *Journal of Revenue and Pricing Management*. doi:10.1057/s41272-019-00220-7.

Guillotin, B., & Mangematin, V. (2015). Internationalization strategies of business schools: How flat is the world? *Thunderbird International Business Review*, *57*(5), 343–357. doi:10.1002/tie.21705.

Gupta, H., & Singhal, N. (2017). Framework for embedding sustainability in business schools: A review. *Vision: The Journal of Business Perspective*, *21*(2), 195–203. doi:10.1177/0972262917700993.

Halkias, D. (2011a). *Editorial:* 'How do we get to the highly entrepreneurial society?' *International Journal of Social Entrepreneurship and Innovation*, *1*(2), 121–123.

Halkias, D. (2011b). *Book review:* 'Scaling social impact: New thinking'. *International Journal of Social Entrepreneurship and Innovation*, *1*(2), 213–214.

Halkias, D. (2011c). *Editorial:* 'For social innovation, it's time for entrepreneurs to deviate from the plan…'. *International Journal of Social Entrepreneurship and Innovation*, *1*(1), 1–3.

Halkias, D., Harkiolakis, N., & Komodromos, M. (2017). A historical view of leadership prototypes: Looking backwards to move forward. *International Leadership Journal*, *9*(3), 6–23.

Halkias, D., Katsioloudes, M., Clayton, G., Mills, G., & Caracatsanis, S. (2009). The strategic value of AACSB international accreditation in start-up overseas American business schools: Two case studies. *The International Journal of Business Innovation and Research*, *3*(2), 151–167.

Halkias, D., Santora, J., Harkiolakis, N., & Thurman, P. (2017). *Leadership and change management: A cross-cultural perspective*. London: Routledge/Taylor Francis.

Halkias, D., & Thurman, P. (2012). Entrepreneurship and sustainability: Can business really alleviate poverty? *International Journal of Social Entrepreneurship and Innovation*, *1*(4), 419–427.

Halkias, D., & Thurman, P. W. (2016). *Entrepreneurship and sustainability: Business solutions for poverty alleviation from around the world*. New York, NY: Routledge.

Harkiolakis, N., Halkias, D., & Abadir, S. (2012). *E-negotiation: Social networking and cross-cultural business transactions*. London: Gower Publishers.

Hill, A. (2018, January 25). *Technology, globalisation and the squeeze on good jobs*. Retrieved September 18, 2018, from https://www.ft.com/content/e66b2fa0-f7ca-11e7-a4c9-bbdefa4f210b.

Horn, M. B., & Dunagan, A. (2018). Innovation and quality assurance in higher education. Clayton Christensen Institute for Disruptive Innovation, June 26, 2018. Retrieved October 21, 2018, from https://www.christensen institute.org/publications/quality-assurance/.

Hu, E. Y. (2017). *Do undergraduate business schools cultivate creative thinking: The Wharton curriculum as a case in point* (Undergraduate thesis). Retrieved September 18, 2018, from http://repository.upenn.edu/joseph_ wharton_scholars/27.

Hubbard, G. (2019, April 22). *The real value of business schools. BizEd Magazine*. Retrieved November 20, 2019, from https://bized.aacsb.edu/articles/ 2019/may/the-real-value-of-business-schools.

Hühn, M. P. (2014). You reap what you sow: How MBA programs undermine ethics. *Journal of Business Ethics, 121*(4), 527–541. doi:10.1007/s10551-013-1733-z.

Hunter, S. M., & Halkias, D. (2016). The psychosocial impact of mobile social networking among young adults in Jamaica. *International Journal of Technology Enhanced Learning, 8*(3/4), 264–278.

IMD Business School. (2019a). *Why IMD?* Retrieved November 25, 2019, from https://www.imd.org/why-imd/about-imd/?utm_medium=search-rem&utm_ source=Google&utm_campaign=AD_SEREM_Brand.

IMD Business School. (2019b). *Why IMD?* Retrieved November 25, 2019, from https://www.imd.org/why-imd/sustainability/policy-principles/?utm_ medium=search-rem&utm_source=Google&utm_campaign=AD_ SEREM_Brand.

Irani, Z. (2015). *Opening doors for doctorates*. BizEd, July 1. Retrieved November 16, 2019, from https://bized.aacsb.edu/articles/2015/07/opening-doors-for-doctorates.

Iversen, J. S. (2006). Futures thinking methodologies and options for education. In *Think Scenarios, Rethink Education* (pp. 107–120). Paris, France: OECD Publishing. doi:10.1787/9789264023642-8-en.

Jack, A. (2019, October 21). *Business schools work towards a better world*. Retrieved November 20, 2019, from https://www.ft.com/content/cee526b6-e444-11e9-b112-9624ec9edc59.

Jogunola, O., & Varis, K. (2018). The evaluation of internationalization strategies of Finnish universities: A case study of two universities in Finland. *Journal of Higher Education Theory and Practice, 18*(6). doi:10.33423/jhetp. v18i6.152.

Kamel, S. (2012). *Entrepreneurial uprising*. BizEd, November 4. Retrieved November 15, 2019, from https://bized.aacsb.edu/articles/2012/11/entrepreneurial-uprising.

Kanaan, F., & Azad, B. (2019). *Scaling up SMEs*. BizEd, October 31. Retrieved November 14, 2019, from https://bized.aacsb.edu/articles/2019/ november/scaling-up-smes.

Kaplan, A. M. (2018). A school is "a building that has four walls...with tomorrow inside": Toward the reinvention of the business school. *Business Horizons, 61*(4), 599–608. doi:10.1016/j.bushor.2018.03.010.

Khare, A., & Hurst, D. (Eds). (2018). *On the line – Business education in the digital age.* Cham, Switzerland: Springer International Publishing AG. doi:10.1007/978-3-319-62776-2.

King, A. A., & Baatartogtokh, B. (2015). How useful is the theory of disruptive innovation? *MIT Sloan Management Review, 57*(1), 77.

Komodromos, M., & Halkias, D. (2015). *Organizational justice during strategic change: The employee's perspective.* London: Gower Publishers.

Kong, S. C., Wong, T. L., Tang, M., Chow, C. F., & Tse, K. H. (Eds). (2017). *Emerging practices in scholarship of learning and teaching in a digital era.* Singapore: Springer Nature Singapore Pte Ltd.

Kreibich, R., Oertel, B., & Wölk, M. (2012). *Futures studies and future-oriented technology analysis principles, methodology and research questions.* HIIG Discussion Paper Series No. 2012-05. doi:10.2139/ssrn.2094215.

Krishnan, D. (2019, April 25). *How business schools can change the world.* Retrieved November 20, 2019, from https://www.strategy-business.com/blog/How-business-schools-can-change-the-world.

Lanteri, A. (2019). *CLEVER: The six strategic drivers for the fourth industrial revolution.* Austin, TX: Lioncrest Publishing.

Lanteri, A., Giordano, F., & Michelini, L. (2017). Social incubators as socially entrepreneurial initiatives. In *Academy of Management Proceedings* (Vol. 2017, No. 1, p. 15229). Briarcliff Manor, NY: Academy of Management.

LeBlanc, P. J. (2018). Higher education in a VUCA world. *Change: The Magazine of Higher Learning, 50*(3–4), 23–26.

Le Breton-Miller, I., & Miller, D. (2008). To grow or to harvest? Governance, strategy and performance in family and lone founder firms. *Journal of Strategy and Management, 1*(1), 41–56.

Leiber, N. (2019, November 4). *Business school students are putting the planet before profits.* Retrieved November 20, 2019, from https://www.bloomberg.com/news/articles/2019-11-04/more-mba-students-want-sustainability-programs.

Leonhard, G. (2014). *Understanding and embracing digital transformation: The future of business, commerce and society.* Retrieved December 12, 2018, from https://www.futuristgerd.com/old_lib/2014/09/digital-transformation-future-of-business-and-commerce-gerd-leonhard-speaker-futurist-web.pdf.

Lessa, B. D. S., Spier, K. F., & Do Nascimento, L. F. M. (2018). Barriers to sustainability in management schools: A Bourdieusian explanation. *Administração: Ensino e Pesquisa, 19*(3), 555–582.

Longmore, A.-L., Grant, G., & Golnaraghi, G. (2018). Closing the 21st-century knowledge gap: Reconceptualizing teaching and learning to transform business education. *Journal of Transformative Education, 16*(3), 1–23. doi:10.1177/1541344617738514.

Lorange, P. (2012). The business school of the future: The network-based business model. *Journal of Management Development, 31*(4), 424–430. doi:10.1108/02621711211219077.

Lorange, P. (2013). Business school culture: Customer-focused, virtual and cooperative. *Education + Training, 55*(4/5), 336–347. doi:10.1108/004009113 11325992.

Lorange, P., & Thomas, H. (2016). Pedagogical advances in business models at business schools – in the age of networks. *Journal of Management Development, 35*(7), 889–900. doi:10.1108/jmd-11-2014-0150.

Markides, C. (2006). Disruptive innovation: In need of better theory. *Journal of Product Innovation Management, 23*(1), 19–25.

Mescon, T. (2019). *Middle East and North Africa Affinity Group guides impact through case studies.* AACSB International, January 16. Retrieved November 14, 2019, from https://www.aacsb.edu/blog/2019/january/middle-east-north-africa-affinity-group-guides-impact-through-case-studies.

Millar, C. C., Groth, O., & Mahon, J. F. (2018). Management innovation in a VUCA world: Challenges and recommendations. *California Management Review.* doi:10.1177/0008125618805111.

Mingers, J. (2015). Helping business schools engage with real problems: The contribution of critical realism and systems thinking. *European Journal of Operational Research, 242*(2015), 316–331. doi:10.1016/j.ejor.2014.10.058.

Minocha, S., Reynolds, M., & Hristov, D. (2017). Developing imaginators not managers – How to flip the business school model. *The International Journal of Management Education, 15*(3), 481–489. doi:10.1016/j.ijme.2017.08.002.

Montgomery, L., & Neylon, C. (2018, September 17). *In a globalised and networked world, what is the unique value a university can bring? Introducing Open Knowledge Institutions.* Retrieved October 11, 2018, from http://blogs.lse.ac.uk/impactofsocialsciences/2018/09/17/in-a-globalised-and-networked-world-what-is-the-unique-value-a-university-can-bring-introducing-open-knowledge-institutions/.

Moules, J. (2019, October 20). *MBA students seek higher 'purpose' than mere money.* Retrieved November 20, 2019, from https://www.ft.com/content/5ee78ac2-e456-11e9-b112-9624ec9edc59.

Murcia, M. J., Rocha, H. O., & Birkinshaw, J. (2018). Business schools at the crossroads? A trip back from Sparta to Athens. *Journal of Business Ethics, 150*(2), 579–591. doi:10.1007/s10551-016-3129-3.

Murray, S. (2019, October 20). *Jobseekers want employers to commit to meaningful social impact.* Retrieved November 20, 2019, from https://www.ft.com/content/39d1367c-e445-11e9-b112-9624ec9edc59.

Nandan, S., Halkias, D., Thurman, P., Komodromos, M., & Alserhan, B. (2018). Assessing cross-national invariance of the three-component model of organizational commitment: A cross-country study of university faculty. *EuroMed Journal of Business, 13*(3), 254–279.

Neal, M. (2017). Learning from poverty: Why business schools should address poverty, and how they can go about it. *Academy of Management Learning & Education, 16*(1), 54–69. doi:10.5465/amle.2014.0369.

Neubert, M. (2014). *Global market strategies: How to turn your company into a successful international enterprise.* Frankfurt, Germany: Campus Verlag.

Neubert, M. (2016). Significance of the speed of internationalisation for born global firms – A multiple case study approach. *International Journal of Teaching and Case Studies, 7*(1), 66–81. doi:10.1504/IJTCS.2016.076067.

Neubert, M. (2017a). International pricing strategies for born-global firms. *Central European Business Review, 6*(3), 41–50. doi:10.18267/j.cebr.185.

Neubert, M. (2017b). Lean internationalization: How to globalise early and fast in a small economy. *Technology Innovation Management Review, 7*(5), 16–22. doi:10.22215/timreview/1073.

Neubert, M. (2018a). Internationalisation behaviour of small and medium-sized enterprises from emerging markets: Implications for sustainability. *Latin American Journal of Management for Sustainable Development, 4*(3), 226–238. doi:10.1504/LAJMSD.2018.096072.

Neubert, M. (2018b). The impact of digitalization on the speed of internationalization of lean global startups. *Technology Innovation Management Review, 8*(5), 44–54. doi:10.22215/timreview/1158.

Neubert, M., & Van Der Krogt, A. (2017). Lean internationalisation of high-tech firms. *International Journal of Teaching and Case Studies, 8*(2/3), 133–150. doi:10.1504/IJTCS.2017.086679.

Neubert, M., & Van Der Krogt, A. (2018). Impact of business intelligence solutions on export performance of software firms in emerging economies. *Technology Innovation Management Review, 8*(9), 39–49. doi:10.22215/timreview/1185.

Neubert, M., & Van der Krogt, A. (2019). Decision-makers impact on the internationalization of high-technology firms in emerging markets. *Journal of Global Entrepreneurship Research.* doi:10.1186/s40497-019-0195-x.

Newbigin, J. (2017). *New and changing dynamics: How the global creative economy is evolving.* Retrieved December 12, 2018, from https://creativeconomy.britishcouncil.org/media/resources/BC_CE_New_and_Changing_Dynamics_2017.pdf.

Nickisch, C. (Presenter). (2018, February 14). *The future of MBA education* [Audio podcast]. Retrieved September 17, 2018, from https://hbr.org/ideacast/2018/02/the-future-of-mba-education.

Nilsson, P. (2018a, September 11). *Do MBA courses teach the right skills? Readers respond.* Retrieved September 18, 2018, from https://www.ft.com/content/ebc59d3c-b1c9-11e8-99ca-68cf89602132.

Nilsson, P. (2018b, September 3). *What top employers want from MBA graduates.* Retrieved September 18, 2018, from https://www.ft.com/content/64b19e8e-aaa5-11e8-89a1-e5de165fa619.

Page, M. J., Brunsveld, N., & Bevelander, D. L. (2017). Does international business accreditation assure quality or constrain innovation? *Business Education & Accreditation, 9*(2), 15–26.

Painter-Morland, M., & Slegers, R. (2018). Strengthening "giving voice to values" in business schools by reconsidering the "invisible hand" metaphor. *Journal of Business Ethics, 147*(4), 807–819. doi:10.1007/s10551-017-3506-6.

Peters, K., Smith, R. R., & Thomas, H. (2018). *Rethinking the business models of business schools: A critical review and change agenda for the future.* Bingley, UK: Emerald Publishing Limited. doi:10.1108/9781787548749.

Peters, K., Thomas, H., & Smith, R. R. (2018). The business of business schools. *Global Focus: The EFMD Business Magazine, 12*(1), 6–11.

Pitt-Watson, D., & Quigley, E. (2019). *Business school rankings for the 21st century.* Retrieved from United Nations Global Compact website: https://www.unglobalcompact.org/library/5654.

Press, G. (2019, October 29). *Top 10 tech predictions for 2020 from IDC.* Retrieved November 20, 2019, from https://www-forbes com.cdn. ampproject.org/c/s/www.forbes.com/sites/gilpress/2019/10/29/top-10-tech-predictions-for-2020-from-idc/amp/.

Robinson, S. (2018). *Academic view: What "sustainability" means in an MBA curriculum.* Retrieved October 1, 2018, from https://www.economist.com/node/21745910.

Schlegelmilch, B. B., & Thomas, H. (2011). The MBA in 2020: Will there still be one? *Journal of Management Development, 30*(5), 474–482. doi:10.1108/02621711111132984.

Schoemaker, P. J. H. (2008). The future challenges of business: Rethinking management education. *California Management Review, 50*(3), 119–139. doi:10.2307/41166448.

Schwab, K. (2016). *The Fourth Industrial Revolution: What it means and how to respond.* Retrieved January 2, 2019, from https://www.weforum.org/agenda/2016/01/the-fourth-industrial-revolution-what-it-means-and-how-to-respond/.

Schwab, K. (2017). *The fourth industrial revolution.* New York, NY: Crown Business.

Schworm, S. K., Cadin, L., Carbone, V., Festing, M., Leon, E., & Muratbekova-Touron, M. (2017). The impact of international business education on career success — Evidence from Europe. *European Management Journal, 35*(4), 493–504. doi:10.5465/ambpp.2015.133.

Shinn, S. (2012, May 1). *Developing the world.* BizEd Magazine. Retrieved November 20, 2019, from https://bized.aacsb.edu/articles/2012/05/developing-the-world.

Shinn, S. (2018). *Ready, set, accelerate.* BizEd, November 1. Retrieved November 15, 2019, from https://bized.aacsb.edu/articles/2018/11/ready-set-accelerate.

Shinn, S. (2019, July 3). *Poised to pivot.* BizEd Magazine. Retrieved November 20, 2019, from https://bized.aacsb.edu/articles/2019/july/poised-to-pivot.

Stoten, D. W. (2018). Reforming the MBA: A survey of elite British universities. *Journal of Management Development, 37*(5), 397–408. doi:10.1108/JMD-08-2017-0264.

Tett, G. (2019, October 20). *US business schools realise ESG is no fad but part of long-term trend.* Retrieved November 20, 2019, from https://www.ft.com/content/55c0472c-e45b-11e9-b112-9624ec9edc59.

The Economist. (2019, November 2). *American business schools are reinventing the MBA.* Retrieved November 20, 2019, from https://www.economist.com/business/2019/11/02/american-business-schools-are-reinventing-the-mba.

Thomas, H., & Cornuel, E. (2012). Business schools in transition? Issues of impact, legitimacy, capabilities and re-invention. *Journal of Management Development, 31*(4), 329–335. doi:10.1108/02621711211219095.

Thomas, H., Lorange, P., & Sheth, J. (2013). *The business school in the twenty-first century: Emergent challenges and new business models.* Cambridge, UK: Cambridge University Press.

Thomas, H., Lorange, P., & Sheth, J. (2014a). Dynamic capabilities and the business school of the future. *Global Focus: The EFMD Business Magazine, 8*(1), 6–11.

Thomas, H., Lorange, P., & Sheth, J. (2014b). The business school of the future. *EFMD Global Focus, 8*(1), 1–79.

Tse, T. C. M., & Esposito, M. (2017, March 11). *Understanding how the future unfolds: Using drive to harness the power of today's megatrends.* Austin, TX: Lioncrest Publishing.

Tse, T. C. M., Esposito, M., & Goh, D. (2019, June 4). *The AI republic: Building the nexus between humans and intelligent automation.* Austin, TX: Lioncrest Publishing.

Üçok Hughes, M., Upadhyaya, S., & Houston, R. (2019). Educating future corporate managers for a sustainable world: Recommendations for a paradigm shift in business education. *On the Horizon, 26*(3), 194–205. doi:10.1108/OTH-01-2018-0007.

United Nations. (2015). *Transforming our world: The 2030 Agenda for Sustainable Development.* Retrieved November 20, 2019, from https://sustainabledevelopment.un.org/content/documents/21252030%20Agenda%20for%20Sustainable%20Development%20web.pdf.

Upadhyaya, S., Hughes, M. Ü., & Houston, H. R. (2019). Using sustainability as a framework for marketing curricula and pedagogy. *The Journal of Sustainability Education, 20*, 19 p. ISSN: 2151-7452. Retrieved December 18, 2019, from http://www.susted.com/wordpress/content/using-sustainability-as-a-framework-for-marketing-curricula-and-pedagogy_2019_04/.

Wiraeus, D., & Creelman, J. (2019). *Agile strategy management in the digital age: How dynamic balanced scorecards transform decision making, speed and effectiveness.* Cham, Switzerland: Palgrave Macmillan. doi:10.1007/978-3-319-76309-5.

World Economic Forum. (2017). *Realizing the potential of blockchain – A multistakeholder approach to the stewardship of blockchain and cryptocurrencies.* Retrieved December 12, 2018, from http://www3.weforum.org/docs/WEF_Realizing_Potential_Blockchain.pdf.

Yesufu, L. O. (2018). Motives and measures of higher education internationalisation: A case study of a Canadian university. *International Journal of Higher Education, 7*(2), 155–168.

Index

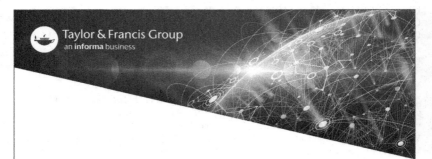

Printed in the United States
by Baker & Taylor Publisher Services